ARCHITECTURE REBORN

THE CONVERSION AND RECONSTRUCTION OF OLD BUILDINGS

ARCHIT

REBORN

ECTURE

THE CONVERSION AND RECONSTRUCTION OF OLD BUILDINGS

KENNETH POWELL

LAURENCE KING

CONTEN

T S

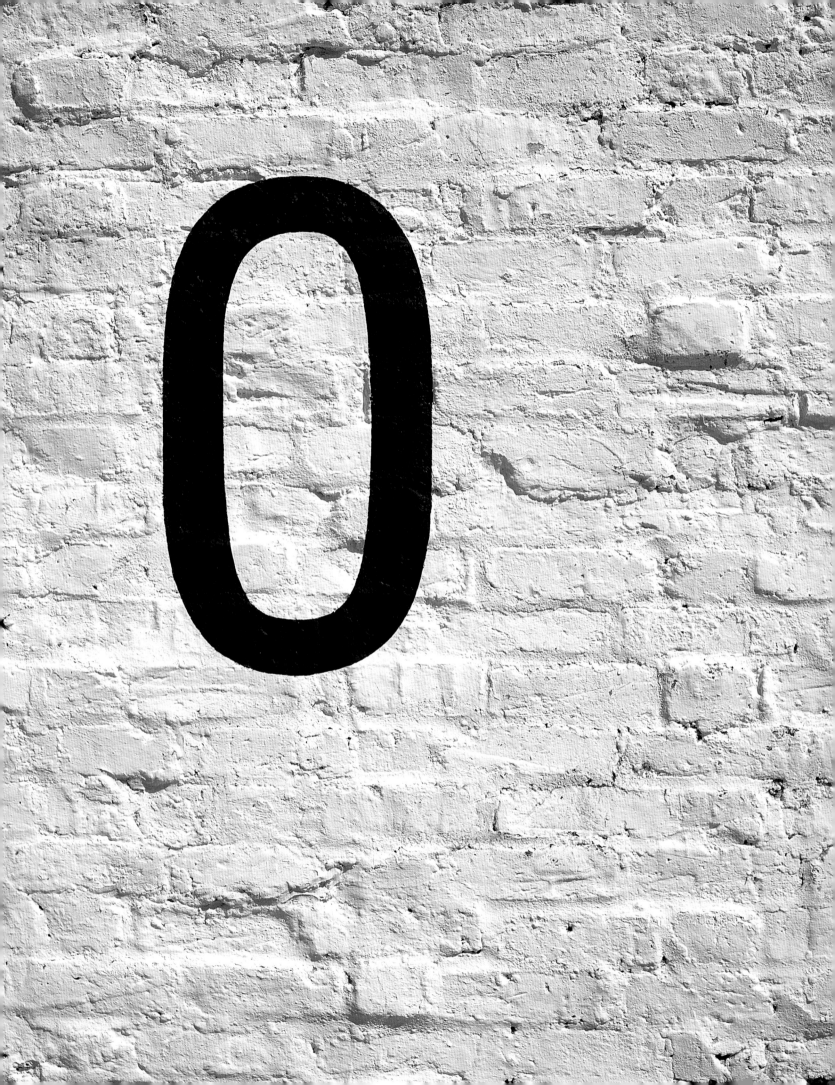

INTRODUCTION

Andrea Palladio, Basilica Palladiana, Vicenza, 1549–1617

BUILDINGS AND CHANGE: PERMANENCE AND TRANSFORMATION

The history of the buildings that the human race has created over thousands of years is one of constant change. Political, religious and economic regimes rise and fall; buildings, more often than not, outlast civilizations. Greek and Roman temples became Christian churches, English monasteries were recycled as country houses and Russian palaces became post-Revolution museums of the people. More recently, nineteenth-century American mills and railway stations have been turned into shopping malls and hotels.

Today, office and industrial buildings of the 1950s and 1960s are being recast for domestic and 'leisure' use – for the simple reason that conversion is a cheaper and less complicated process than new-build. The Georgian-built West End of London is no longer a residential enclave, but many of its streets and squares survive as locations for prestige offices and medical consulting rooms. Old buildings are remarkably resilient. The Marais district of Paris was a fashionable *quartier* of private palaces in the eighteenth century. By the early years of the twentieth century, it was a rundown slum, on the road to clearance. Now it is fashionable once more, a modish place to live and a cultural quarter which is a favourite destination for tourists.

Reusing existing buildings is, first and foremost, a matter of common-sense economics and it is a process which has gone on throughout history. Building conversion often took place, in the past, without regard for history or 'character'. There are numerous examples: the Roman amphitheatre in Lucca was simply absorbed into the urban fabric, with houses built into its raked structure and the open centre filled with new buildings: only in the nineteenth century was the monument 'rediscovered' by archaeologists. The nave of the medieval abbey at Malmesbury, Wiltshire was subdivided at the Reformation for use as a clothing factory. In the sixteenth century, Palladio completely engulfed the ancient Palazzo Publico in Vicenza in his new Basilica [1]. Many of the *hôtels particuliers* (private mansions) of Paris were ruthlessly cut up into small apartments. Ordinary houses were often re-faced over the centuries: an eighteenth-century brick or stucco frontage may conceal a medieval timber frame.

The driving force behind reuse was, in other words, functional and financial. Only in the nineteenth century did legislation, rooted in a romantic and historicist philosophy, begin to emerge with the aim of protecting old buildings. In France, the state took an early lead. In Britain, prolonged voluntary effort, under the leadership of William Morris, founder of the Society for the Protection of Ancient Buildings (SPAB), and inspired by the writings of John Ruskin, was necessary before the authorities would act to limit the rights of private owners. It was well into the twentieth century before American states and cities were persuaded to do likewise – even today, immense disparities prevail between the approach to the landmark preservation of, for example, Los Angeles and that of New York City.

The Western concept of 'heritage' still means little in Far Eastern countries and the Ruskinian notion of an irreplaceable imprint of the past, contained within the fabric of an old building, means virtually nothing to, say, the Japanese. In Japan, ancient temples have been regularly rebuilt over the centuries to ensure the survival of their form, rather than their actual fabric. In the West nonetheless, historic buildings legislation, based on a complex mix of historicist, didactic, nationalistic, nostalgic and even moral precepts, is now virtually universal. In Britain, there are over 500,000 listed buildings; two-thirds of the City of Westminster, at the heart of London, is protected by conservation areas. The historic centres of Italian cities are safeguarded by controls that cover buildings and streets in minute detail. It is more than 60 years since the Congrès Internationaux d'Architecture Moderne (CIAM), led by Le Corbusier and Sigfried Giedion, projected the demolition of much of central Paris. Today, Corbusier would probably find it difficult to build there at all.

THE MODERN MOVEMENT AND AFTER

Corbusier's architectural vision was rooted in a dynamic view of the world, itself the outcome of the First World War and part of a cultural revolution that produced cubist and surrealist art forms, the writings of Joyce and Kafka and the music of Stravinsky and Berg [2]. To Corbusier and his contemporaries, the old cities of Europe seemed to be mausolea of a dead culture. In the USA, Frank Lloyd Wright planned new Prairie cities, low-rise and dependent on the automobile. Modern architecture, it was assumed, would re-make the world. That dream ended with the Second World War, though few knew it at the time.

The post-war building boom was a triumph for modernism, but it produced a backlash. The failure of many new social housing schemes (in the USA, Pruitt-Igoe; in Britain, Ronan Point) were symbols of the breakdown of the modernist dream. Disillusionment with the destructive approach to town planning typical of the period led to popular pressure for a new direction. Jane Jacobs's seminal book *Death and Life of Great American Cities* (1961) insisted that 'ordinary' buildings, as well as landmarks, needed to be preserved – modernist planning had disregarded the organic qualities of the city. Cities needed old buildings, Jacobs insisted. 'By old buildings I mean not museum-piece old buildings... but also a lot of plain, ordinary, low-value old buildings, including some rundown old buildings.' [1]

The oil crisis of the 1970s provided the backbone to a burgeoning ecological

2

Le Corbusier, Plan for a modern city, 1922

3

McKim, Mead & White, Pennsylvania Station, New York, 1902–11

movement which insisted that demolition equalled waste. A decade earlier, modern architects came to the fore in preservationist campaigns. These included Peter and Alison Smithson in the campaign to save London's Euston Arch (alongside the poet John Betjeman, who had been a prominent supporter of modern architecture) and Philip Johnson, with Jackie Kennedy and others, in the battle for New York's Pennsylvania Station [3]. Neither of these campaigns was successful. Nor was that for Paris's Les Halles, which won the support of many French architects and of Renzo Piano and Richard Rogers, who were beginning to build the Pompidou Centre nearby and greatly admired the iron and glass market halls (in the same tradition as their own work). The Euston Arch, Penn Station and Les Halles were, however, landmarks in the rise of conservation. In each case, mediocre new developments replaced lost masterworks, providing an obvious moral for the future. When London's St Pancras station, New York's Grand Central Terminal and the Marais in Paris came under threat, all were 'saved'. Public opinion had changed.

While Corbusier's Modern Movement rhetoric had not generally prevailed (most of modernism's key monuments were built within the context of existing towns and cities), for many architects and critics trained before the Second World War, the new conservationist mood was irritating. John Summerson feared that 'dictatorship in preservation... may easily become a kind of national ritual, an inglorious fetishism'.[2] But architecture functions as a business, and architects had to adapt to prevailing attitudes and learn to work with existing buildings and cities. In the 1980s and 1990s, moreover, working with 'old' buildings – which sometimes date, in fact, from the 1960s – has become a key element in architectural practice. A recent survey revealed that over 70 per cent of the current workload of American architects was concerned with reuse.

Out of necessity comes invention, and conversion and rehabilitation schemes now generate some of the most innovative and intelligent work, by architects such as Frank Gehry, Bernard Tschumi, Norman Foster, Enric Miralles, Eric Owen Moss and Herzog & de Meuron. 'Saving' old buildings is no longer enough. The aim is not preservation but transformation, an architectural, rather than a sentimental or historicist approach to creating new form out of old fabric.

THE POLITICS OF PRESERVATION

Buildings indelibly embody the ideologies of the culture that shapes them. In some cases, new uses involve the attenuation or removal of existing symbolism, such as painting over the mosaics of Hagia Sophia (which converted easily from church to mosque) by the Turkish conquerors of Constantinople. Early

conversions of nineteenth-century industrial buildings tended to erase or dilute their functional ambience, since, until very recently, the associations of industry (such as noise, pollution and bad working conditions) were negative. Today, however, there are increasingly few people who remember mill life as it was.

Preservation, as Summerson pointed out, is an irrational urge, stemming from a deep psychological need for security and 'roots'. Architectural conservationists see historic buildings as a threatened species, to be protected not only from destruction but equally from injury and maltreatment. They traditionally see themselves as crusaders. (The photographer Richard Nickel, 1928–72, killed in the ruins of Louis Sullivan's Chicago Stock Exchange, was one of the few actual martyrs of the movement.[3]) Architects may be praised for 'making something' of an ordinary old building – though, perhaps, attacked for 'gentrifying' it – but too often they are damned for any attempt to alter the character of a historic monument.

Attitudes to refurbishment and alteration vary from country to country. The idea of old buildings as inviolate holds most sway in Britain, where modern ideas about preservation were forged by Ruskin and Morris. Ironically, both of these prophetic figures valued old buildings because they bore 'the mark of man', the impact of successive generations, and strongly opposed 'restoration', which supposedly intended to 'purify' buildings. They accepted that buildings must change as societies change – both were, in their ways, advocates of radical social transformation. Ruskin and Morris insisted that imitating past styles was an insult rather than a compliment to the builders of the past: every generation should build according to the needs and manners of its own age. Ruskin argued that, in an extreme case of disrepair, it might be preferable to demolish an old building and replace it with an 'honest' modern structure rather than attempt 'false' restoration. Morris saw conservation as linked to the cause of modernity, encouraging creativity rather than the imitation of the past. Seemingly, the current direction of transformation is in tune with the ideas originating from these pioneers of the modern conservation movement.

The roots of transformation as an architectural concern (without preservation as a motivation) lie in the nineteenth century and with the 'restorers', such as Sir George Gilbert Scott in England and Viollet-le-Duc in France, whom Ruskin and Morris so despised. The best Gothic Revivalists were able to work in the spirit of the original, while making use of modern materials and techniques where appropriate. But their work to churches and cathedrals was guided by an in-built reverence for the Middle Ages. Twentieth-century architects reveal a different agenda, based on a respect for the past but a total lack of

Carlo Scarpa, Fondazione Querini-Stampalia, Venice, 1963

Chareau and Bijvoet, Maison de Verre, Paris, 1932

deference. Gunnar Asplund's extension to the Gothenburg courthouse, for example, a well-loved monument at the core of the old city, boldly rejected pastiche in favour of a new building which externally echoes the proportions and rhythms of its neighbour without any use of historic detail. Behind the façade, the architecture is entirely modern and the new and old are kept clearly distinct.

The Roots of Transformation

In post-war Italy, a more radical approach to transformation emerged. The work of Carlo Scarpa (1906–78) has acquired a particular resonance for many late twentieth-century practitioners of transformation. Born in Venice – most of his work was in the city or surrounding region – Scarpa always preferred adding to existing buildings rather than designing new structures, a predilection which his contemporaries found odd, even perverse. In response, Scarpa cited the inspiration of the great architects of the past: Brunelleschi's masterpiece, the dome of the Duomo in Florence, was an addition to an existing building. Did this diminish its significance – or magnify it? Like Brunelleschi, Scarpa refused to design in past styles and his work was a constant dialogue with history. Museum design was a particular speciality. Scarpa's reconstruction of the Castelvecchio at Verona (1956–64) is the best known of his museum projects and involved unpicking an earlier, historicist restoration done in the 1920s, when the fortress first became a museum. At that time, the emphasis was on conversion. Scarpa wished to transform the building and with it the visitor's encounter with the works of art it contained. He juxtaposed old work with new, using an extraordinary palette of materials – concrete, stone, steel, bronze, timber and plaster – and capitalized on the great variety of spaces within the *castello*, regarding the proper use of natural light as a prime ingredient in the display of objects.

Scarpa's concern for dramatizing the history of a building is seen to spectacular effect in the famous Cangrande space, where he demolished a section of the fabric to expose the layers within. The equestrian statue of Cangrande della Scala stands on a heavy concrete beam, deliberately set askew, under a new roof, itself terminating in a jagged gable. In this work, Scarpa prefigures not only a shift in approach to new and old, unintelligible to the original Modern Movement thinkers, but equally the demonstrative, even bloody-minded technique of late twentieth-century architects for whom the past is neither irrelevant nor something to be blindly reverenced. At the Fondazione Querini-Stampalia in Venice, Scarpa used the opportunity provided by a water-logged ground floor to thread a new level through the historic palazzo, allowing the canal to penetrate the building and form an internal moat [4]. The bridge Scarpa

designed to provide access across a small canal has become an icon of historical inspiration, rooted in Venetian precedents but entirely modern.

The magnitude of Scarpa's achievement does not detract from the significance of other work in the same vein by his contemporaries. A close parallel for the Castelvecchio is provided by the somewhat earlier (and no less notable) reconstruction of the Castello Sforza in Milan by the practice BBPR (Banfi, Belgiojoso, Peressutti & Rogers). Equally numinous was the work of Franco Albini – for example, in the refurbishment of the Palazzo Bianco in Genoa as a picture gallery, following severe damage to the building in the Second World War. More recently, the Palazzo della Pilotta in Parma, which also suffered serious war damage, has been transformed by Guido Canali into a major art museum. Canali takes visitors into the museum through the restored Farnese Theatre. From the ground floor, they ascend steadily via bridges and walkways suspended within the vast space of the old building, which is detached from the new work but always present. Albani, Helg & Piva's phased conversion (1969–85) of a former monastery to house the Civic Museum in Padua is externally discreet, but displays the usual Italian concern for dramatic display of artefacts. The work of Gae Aulenti is also within this transformational tradition, though her best-known museum project, the Musée d'Orsay in Paris, lacks the elegance of her best Italian work.

The interface of old and new is a constant theme in twentieth-century Italian architecture. Once literal historicism was cast aside after the First World War, Italian architects had to confront the weight of history in a more sophisticated way. This new approach is seen, for example, in the work of Ignazio Gardella, whose apartment block on the Zattere in Venice (1954–58) is a model of questioning contextualism. Later in his career, Gardella worked with Aldo Rossi on the bold reconstruction of the war-damaged San Carlo opera house in Genoa, a project which is as notable for its urban preoccupations as for its resuscitation of a great cultural institution.

Like Scarpa, Pierre Chareau (1883–1950) is one of the most frequently quoted sources among architects of the post-war generation, on the strength of just one project, the Maison de Verre in Paris (1928–32) [5]. With the gynaecologist Jean Dalsace and his wife as clients and the Dutch architect Bernard Bijvoet as collaborator, Chareau gouged out the innards of an eighteenth-century house in the rue St Guillaume (leaving a top-floor tenant, who refused to move out, in residence throughout). He inserted a new steel-framed structure into the void, leaving the steelwork exposed and even celebrating it with colour. In place of a maze of old rooms, Chareau created a magnificent space for modern living at

Rouse Company, South Street Seaport, Manhattan, 1986

piano nobile level, with consulting rooms for Dalsace's practice below. The Maison de Verre used to be seen as a rogue work, with no obvious lessons for the future. Its rediscovery after the Second World War, notably by Richard Rogers and Norman Foster, led to its re-evaluation. (Rogers' own house in London, a total reconstruction within early Victorian façades, was inspired by the Maison de Verre.) Its particular relevance to a modern generation committed to the city and obliged to work with existing urban fabric is obvious.

The work of the German master Hans Döllgast (1891–1974), a classic 'outsider' on the twentieth-century architectural scene, has striking parallels with that of Scarpa. Döllgast's most significant project was the reconstruction of the Alte Pinakothek in Munich, which had been severely damaged by wartime bombing. His work there, which begun in 1946 and continued virtually until the end of his life, eschewed the replication of destroyed historic fabric in favour of a bold but historically-rooted rebuilding. Equally bold were Döllgast's reconstruction and repair schemes for a number of war-ravaged churches in Bavaria. Using both 'traditional' and modern materials, he merged old and new to create moving and often dramatic interiors which bore the scars of history with pride.[4] The cataclysm of the Second World War, which left many German cities devastated, encouraged a ruthlessly honest approach to reconstruction and the rejection of verbatim and 'false' rebuilding.

Gottfried Böhm's rebuilding of the historic Schloss in the centre of Saarbrucken (1982–89) replaced the lost centrepiece with a bold new structure of steel and glass. At Schloss Gotesaue, near Karlsruhe, rebuilt from a gutted shell as a music college by architect Barbara Jakubeit, the exterior was faithfully reinstated. But the interior is modern, tailored to the needs of the present-day users, and culminates in a spectacular crystalline library.

Karljosef Schattner, working in the provincial city of Eichstatt, has similarly rejected pastiche in a number of projects. The conversion of the seventeenth-century Ulmer Hof into a theology faculty and library (1978–80) has turned a former courtyard into a light-filled library, topped by a lightweight, almost matter of fact, steel roof. Schattner's uncompromising approach to transformation, celebrating the old by contrast rather than copying, is seen to striking effect in his last major work, the reconstruction of the Hirschberg Castle as a conference and religious retreat centre.

SAVING THE CITY

Scarpa and Chareau are now regarded as key figures of the post-war European architecture scene. The inspiration of both was the historic European city, a challenge to the radical ideals of modernism. In North America, modernist urban theory was challenged only from the 1960s onwards. Louis Kahn, Robert Venturi and Colin Rowe, complementing the work of Jane Jacobs, argued the case for co-existing with the city. An increasing recognition that American cities were in economic and social decay, with large inner areas becoming impoverished ghettoes for immigrant groups (the film *West Side Story* dramatized the issues for outsiders) led to a change of heart.

Several industrial centres faced terminal decline, including mill towns on the East Coast which had flourished for a century and a half. In larger cities, waterfront and wholesaling areas, made redundant by new freight-handling methods, faced desolation. In Boston, massive redevelopment and an intrusive highway scheme further isolated the waterfront. The once-prosperous 1820s Quincy Market faced abandonment and possible demolition. In the aftermath of the early 1970s oil crisis, however, the city changed direction. Its rehabilitation as a centre for specialist shopping (referred to as a 'festival marketplace') was completed for the American Bicentennial in 1976 by architects Benjamin Thompson Associates. A huge commercial success, the project changed the image of old buildings not only in Boston but throughout the USA. Other formerly obsolete buildings in the area were refurbished rather than demolished, generally in a thorough-going fashion which disturbed European conservationists. (Old windows, doors and other features were torn out and replaced by modern components.) The Rouse Company, which had carried out the Quincy Market scheme, moved on to projects in Baltimore and at South Street Seaport in Manhattan, where museum and retail/restaurant uses were combined in a mix of recycled and new buildings on the model of Quincy Market [6]. (The refurbishment of London's Covent Garden Market in 1980 took its cue from Boston, though there was a more conservationist approach to the treatment of the nineteenth-century buildings.)

The Tax Reform Act approved by Congress in 1976 was a landmark in providing tax incentives for refurbishing old buildings rather than building new and was a natural progression from the preservation legislation of the 1960s. Under the Jimmy Carter presidency, federal funding for preservation initiatives increased ten-fold over a period of a few years, while major cities echoed the new thinking by establishing 'landmark' commissions with powers to protect buildings. (The first successful defence of a 'landmark' in Los Angeles occurred as early as 1962.) Just 48 kilometres (30 miles) from Boston, the town of Lowell, regarded as the cradle of the industrial revolution in America, began to decline between the wars. By the 1970s, this decline looked irreversible and it seemed

Conran Design Partnership, Michelin Building, London, 1987

Stirling Wilford, Tate Gallery, Liverpool, 1988

likely that the great mills would go the way of many others and be reduced to rubble. Lowell's regeneration was achieved by a union of public and private interests, financing the location of new industry (notably computers) and the establishment of a pioneering National Park embracing all the historic industrial sites. From being regarded as valueless, the old mills became assets – Lowell's Market Mills were turned into 230 apartments, together with workshops, galleries and eating places, and reopened in their new role in 1982.

So complete was the change in American attitudes towards old industrial buildings during the 1970s and early 1980s that former factories (such as the Torpedo Factory in Alexandria, Virginia, or the Cannery at Fishermen's Wharf, San Francisco) became prime tourist destinations – as, indeed, did Covent Garden Market in London, once frequented by the fruit and vegetable trade, and now globally famous.

The new interest in 'adaptive reuse' in the USA saw previously ignored and unknown buildings transformed into major landmarks. A prominent example of this process is the former Pensions Building on Judiciary Square in Washington DC. This immense 1880s block now houses the National Building Museum. Its vast central atrium, one of the largest pre-twentieth-century spaces in America, is now a popular venue for government receptions and other prestige social gatherings.

Just as the industrial revolution had been exported from Britain to America, so the recycling revolution crossed the Atlantic in the other direction. When SAVE Britain's Heritage organized its campaigning exhibition *Satanic Mills* in 1979, the British industrial heritage looked acutely threatened. The Thatcherite assault on traditional industry intensified the threat. Entrepreneur-developers, however, such as Ernest Hall and Jonathan Silver, taking the American example to heart, transformed redundant Yorkshire mills, regarded as valueless by the property industry, into thriving and profitable centres for business and tourism. In Leeds and Manchester, derelict riverside warehouses became flats, bars and restaurants. Wigan, long regarded as one of Britain's ugliest towns, developed its own tourist trade by refurbishing a group of canalside warehouses as 'Wigan Pier'. Similar ventures succeeded in northern France, where old textile mills around Lille became housing and shopping complexes. The trauma of the oil crisis had catalyzed a common-sense realization that such buildings were too good to waste. Style-minded residents of converted mills modelled themselves on the artists and media figures who colonized 'lofts' in the SoHo and TriBeCa areas of Manhattan, living in anonymous luxury in buildings which externally looked as they always had done. When the London property market entered a boom period

after the financial 'Big Bang' of 1986, redundant dockland warehouses, of the sort which had been carelessly destroyed only a decade earlier, were bought up by developers for conversion. New Concordia Wharf, developed by entrepreneur Andrew Wadsworth, was an early success. At Butler's Wharf, Sir Terence Conran mixed apartments and shops with a string of new restaurants and a design museum. Conran was also a prime mover in the renovation of the former Michelin Garage, a striking tile-clad art nouveau landmark in South Kensington, as offices, restaurants and space for his Conran Shop [7]. (Although the heavy lid of new rooftop offices jarred, the elegant curtain wall forming the main entrance to the shop provided a good counterpoint to the ornament of the existing structure.) A later Conran venture was the conversion (in 1997) of the listed Bluebird garage on Chelsea's King's Road into a restaurant and retail complex.

By the late-1980s, the commercial potential of sound old buildings was not in question. The increased protection given, particularly to nineteenth-century buildings, by the various systems of listing, scheduling and landmarking further discouraged random demolition. The regenerational value of reuse schemes was also acknowledged. The rescue of the long-threatened Albert Dock in Liverpool, arguably the finest historic dock complex left anywhere, was a boost for the rundown northern port city. The shops there were let and the apartments sold, while Granada Television carried out an immaculate refurbishment of the former office building as its local base. From being a forgotten waste, the Dock became one of the most visited locations in the region. Most of the refurbishment work was conscientious and unobtrusive, but one 12,000 square-metre (40,000 square-foot) block, acquired as the northern branch of the Tate Gallery, was more radically transformed by architects Stirling Wilford [8]. James Stirling had been raised and trained in Liverpool and had always admired the Albert Dock. The use of bold colour in the painting of the building's exterior and in new wall panels and lettering evoked the colours of the shipping lines which once used the Dock. Inside, the construction of a new mezzanine similarly played on a maritime aesthetic. The new Tate bore a distinct Stirling flavour, and came to be seen as a cultural landmark for the north. (The building was expanded and remodelled – and the striking mezzanine removed – by Michael Wilford in 1996–98.)

TRANSFORMATION AND THE NEW ARCHITECTURE
The recognition that reuse was a different issue from repair and restoration – always the preserve of specialist agencies and practices – opened the way for transformation to be integrated into the art of architecture. Past masters like

9

I.M. Pei, Grand Louvre: Richelieu Wing, Paris, 1993

10

Arup Associates, Maltings Concert Hall, Suffolk, England, 1967

Mies van der Rohe, Corbusier, Wright and Berthold Lubetkin had no obvious interest in old buildings (though Alvar Aalto's transformation of a commonplace warehouse into the Finnish Pavilion for the 1939 New York World's Fair was one of his most magical and radical works). Their present-day successors work regularly with the past. On the largest scale, this sea-change is reflected in a project like the Grand Louvre, centrepiece of François Mitterrand's programme of *grands projets* [9].

Design work began in 1983, after I. M. Pei had been selected as architect. Though the Louvre was unquestionably one of the great museums of the world, it had stagnated. Visitor facilities were poor. Storage, conservation and general staff facilities were worse. The museum was cut off from the life of the city. A whole wing (around a third of the total complex) was permanently closed to the public and occupied by the civil servants of the Ministry of Finance. Pei's reconstruction of the Louvre, completed in 1993 with the opening of the Richelieu Wing, set a new agenda for museum projects worldwide. It was not just an expansion, but a transformation, symbolized by the now-famous Pyramid at the centre of the Cour Napoléon – the gateway to a new subterranean heart for the Louvre. In the second phase of the giant project, the Richelieu Wing was completely reconstructed, 'recreated with the regal proportions that it had always pretended to have but which, in fact, had never existed'. As part of this phase, three spectacular internal spaces were created by glazing over internal courtyards (formerly used as parking areas); the Cour Marly, with its dramatically lightweight aluminium and glass roof engineered by Peter Rice, is one of the great interiors of Paris. Pei's imposing court of escalators, connecting the three main exhibition floors, with great circular oculi (a Kahnian device) offering striking views out to the Cour Napoléon and into the Cour Marly, is another memorable element in the scheme. The old Louvre was experienced – and enjoyed by some – as a disjointed series of spaces, almost like separate museums, to be discovered after a number of visits. Now the whole complex opens itself to anyone with the energy to traverse it, while links to underground shopping and car-parking emphasize the fact that it is no longer a place apart.

Museums have been prime catalysts of architectural transformation in the 1980s and 1990s. Norman Foster's project for the British Museum is potentially as dramatic in its effect as Pei's Louvre, while Gae Aulenti's reconstruction of the National Gallery of Catalunya in Barcelona and David Chipperfield's extension scheme for the Neues Museum in Berlin will transform those institutions. (In the latter project, the war-ravaged interior of the great neoclassical building will be fused into a collage with radical new interventions – completion is scheduled for

2003.) The museum building boom of recent decades has produced not just memorable new buildings – such as Frank Gehry's Guggenheim in Bilbao and Richard Meier's Getty in California – but equally imaginative reworkings of existing structures. Gehry's Temporary Contemporary (see pages 128–131) on the fringe of downtown Los Angeles was always intended to close when the permanent Museum of Contemporary Art, designed by Arata Isozaki, opened. (The Temporary Contemporary was installed in a group of old warehouses in time for the 1984 Olympics.) So great was the popularity of the gallery that, three years after its closure, it reopened and has since been renovated and extended. The Temporary Contemporary has always been popular with experimental artists, who are attracted to its ad hoc character. Its location equally appeals to many who find the new business district immediately around the permanent MOCA sterile and intimidating.

Recycled buildings generate a spontaneous excitement that challenges designers of new museums, although the raw material may be unpromising. The San Antonio Museum of Art in Texas was once a brewery, the Reina Sofia Museum in Madrid a hospital, the National Museum of Ireland in Dublin an army barracks and the Centre for Contemporary Art in Grenoble a foundry (albeit housed in a building by Gustave Eiffel). In 1985–90, with Lluis Domènech as architect, the Antoni Tàpies Foundation converted a handsome late nineteenth-century printworks in the centre of Barcelona to house a major collection of Tàpies' art works. The elegant interior of the building was treated respectfully, but the street façade was transformed with the addition of a giant rooftop sculpture, a marker of the new use and an apt symbol of Barcelona's continuing commitment to progressive design. Gae Aulenti's conversion of the former Gare d'Orsay into the Musée d'Orsay (1979–86) raised questions of the appropriateness of putting an art gallery into a train shed – Aulenti's interventions into the great interior space have been widely condemned – but the panache of the project carries the day. London's Imperial War Museum was once a mental hospital, though its considerable grandeur fitted it for a more public role. (The major reconstruction of the Museum in recent years, to designs by Arup Associates, has given it a new heart, with space to display large exhibits, in what was an open court.) Although lamented by some critics as marking a lost opportunity for a new building on one of the most prominent sites in London, the decision to house London's new museum of modern art, a branch of the Tate Gallery, in the former Bankside Power Station (see pages 224–227) has opened the way for the first great transformational museum scheme of the twenty-first century.

The use of old buildings for cultural purposes emphasizes continuity. The

11

Renzo Piano, Molo Quarter redevelopment, Genoa, 1992

12

de Metz Green, loft conversion, London, 1998

Maltings at Snape, Suffolk was always a landmark in the area, but its conversion into a concert hall (by Arup Associates) made it a world cultural landmark as the main base for the Aldeburgh Festival [10]. London's famous Roundhouse, a nineteenth-century engine shed famous in the 1960s and 1970s as a venue for rock music and avant-garde theatre, is being converted by John McAslan & Partners into a children's arts centre. Bernard Tschumi's National Studio for Contemporary Arts (see pages 134–141) in a suburb of Lille is a palimpsest upon a complex of buildings, containing a dance hall, cinema and bars, once loved in the neighbourhood but fallen on hard times. Most of the old buildings were kept and repaired, but the innovative element of the scheme was the great new roof that floats above them, creating what Tschumi calls an 'in between' space, 'a place of fantasies and experiments'. The institution is new, but it holds old memories and transforms them. According to Tschumi, such multifunctional spaces will be 'the urban spaces of the twenty-first century'.[4]

Though originating in a very different architectural ideology, Richard Rogers' proposal for a giant 'wave' of glass over the arts centre at London's South Bank (1994–97) would have created a similarly benign 'inside-out' space, encouraging activities ruled out by the bleak landscape of 1960s concrete roofs and walkways yet retaining all the existing arts buildings. The radicalism of this project offended the sensibilities of those for whom outright preservation is the natural way to show respect to a building, even if the needs of present-day and future users are entirely ignored. Fortunately, this approach commands increasingly diminishing support and is particularly out of place in the context of intractable modern environments such as the South Bank.

Architecture is more commonly becoming a series of events, rather than an accumulation of objects. Tschumi's analysis challenges an object-centred view of architecture which was, for all the rhetoric about change, central to the Modern Movement. The latter dealt in inexorable certainties. Postmodern architectural thought is rooted in the chaotic universe, in unpredictability and chance. Whereas the randomness, untidiness and disorder of the traditional city infuriated Modern Movement reformers like Corbusier, late twentieth-century architects embrace the richness of urban life. A generation ago, the preservation of individual buildings was a campaigning cause. Increasingly, entire areas, including SoHo, TriBeCa, Covent Garden or Dublin's Temple Bar, have been regenerated by a mix of restoration, conversion and new design. Temple Bar was destined for total clearance, with a new bus station planned on the site. The area, reprieved from clearance, has become a showplace for a new Irish architecture which is rooted in postmodern urban philosophy. The 500th anniversary in 1992 of Columbus's

journey to the New World provided the impetus for a major regeneration of the old port area of Genoa [11]. It was the inspiration of Genoa-based Renzo Piano to celebrate the event not just by means of an exhibition but by reviving and renewing a whole urban quarter. The Molo area was in poor condition physically and socially, and had been cut off by the construction of the autostrada in the 1960s, yet it was the ancient heart of the city. Piano's masterplan renovated disused warehouses as exhibition and conference facilities. New buildings formed an equally important part of the plan, which mixed public and private enterprise. An entirely new structure, the Grande Bigo, became the symbol of the regenerated port, yet its form was a reinterpretation, on a greatly enlarged scale, of the traditional derricks used on the wharves of Genoa.

THE CITY REBORN

The rediscovery of the city is a late twentieth-century phenomenon, in combat with the now outmoded notion that the city is a dying species. Hackney, probably the poorest of London's boroughs, now contains more artists' studios than all Paris. Artists need generous quantities of cheap, flexible space. London's Space Studios, founded in 1974, set out to convert redundant industrial buildings into studios. By 1998, it was providing space for over 300 artists on 14 sites, many of them in the East End and including old factories and swimming baths once regarded as valueless.

By the 1990s, however, the artists were facing growing competition from developers who, recognizing the demand for housing in the heart of the city, bought up a wide range of long-undervalued redundant buildings for conversion to lofts (large, flexible living spaces in former industrial buildings), the scenario for a way of life first analysed in Sharon Zukin's *Loft Living* (1982) [12]. Urban regeneration can be controversial. The 'clean-up' of New York's Times Square area was part of the city's conspicuous revival in the 1990s, but some New Yorkers felt that an element of sleaze and low-life was part of the city experience. ('Times Square is dead. Long live Times Square', declared Ada Louise Huxtable.) But sleaze had brought real decay to the heart of Manhattan. The 1,750-seat New Amsterdam theatre on West 42nd Street, opened in 1903 (designed by architects Herts & Tallant), was once regarded as New York's finest theatre and was at one time the home of the Ziegfeld Follies. Converted into a cinema in the 1930s, and subsequently badly mutilated, it closed altogether in 1982 and fell into near-ruin – 75 per cent of the interior decor was lost – typifying the plight of the surrounding area. The $36 million renovation of the New Amsterdam, completed in 1997, involved a partnership of public and private funding – the Walt Disney Company

15

Hardy Holzman Pfeiffer, Central Library, Los Angeles, 1994

Altoon & Porter, Southwestern University Law Library, Los Angeles, 1997

is the new owner – and resulted in a sophisticated mix of exact restoration and imaginative renewal which allowed the history of the building to emerge. Architects Hardy Holzman Pfeiffer (HHP) successfully resisted pressure to restore lost features, so the striking 1930s art deco street front, for example, was retained. 'I will not demolish what is real in favour of making false things that look old', insisted Hugh Hardy.

HHP were also responsible for the regeneration of a key monument in downtown Los Angeles – the Central Library, designed by Bertram Grosvenor Goodhue and completed in 1926 [13]. Although dismissed by Reyner Banham in *Los Angeles* (1971) as an irrelevance, out of step with a city that was, he claimed, about 'unfocused ubiquity', downtown LA (where 350,000 people work) has made a comeback. Goodhue's building, a subtle mix of deco-modern, classical and Spanish colonial motifs by one of the masters of early twentieth-century historicism, had faced possible demolition. During the 1980s, it had been badly damaged by fire and earthquake and was closed for six years from 1987. HHP had been commissioned to restore and extend the building in 1983. The scheme completed ten years later included an immaculate restoration of Goodhue's interiors (particularly notable for their profusion of mural decoration) and the construction of an eight-storey, 30,472 square-metre (328,000 square-foot) extension – four storeys below street level – which has vastly augmented the library's resources and doubled its size. The library has been transformed as a vigorous reassertion of the public realm in a quarter of the city where big business has made inroads in the form of anonymous office towers on Bunker Hill.

Not many years ago, historic preservation was largely a non-issue in Los Angeles. It seemed at odds with the vision of the city as promoted by Banham. The latter was essentially an optimist, but the bleaker visions of social fragmentation as reflected in Mike Davis's *City of Quartz* (1990) came to reality in the riots that characterized the early 1990s. Allowing large segments of the city to gradually transform into poor ghettoes was no longer an acceptable course. The innovative postmodern urbanism of Eric Owen Moss, Morphosis, Frank D. Israel and Frank Gehry assumed a new relevance as a way of making the existing city work.

The conversion of old buildings was central to this approach, as in Gehry's Chiat Day project at Venice Beach – which typifies what Charles Jencks calls 'hetero-architecture', an approach to design that accepts and celebrates urban diversity and breaks down the barriers that lead to riots.[6] In this analysis, Moss's ongoing Culver City project (see pages 88–95), that recycles discarded old buildings, is a blow for the city, just as the glossy Bunker Hill office towers are a

recipe for social collapse.

A series of conversion projects of the early 1990s by Israel Callas Shortridge Associates shows an equal concern for the inherent value of existing urban fabric. Comparatively ordinary old buildings form a canvas for a series of radical interventions, inspired, in the case of the Limelight Productions scheme, by the work of Corbusier and Wright. More conventional is the conversion (by architects Altoon & Porter) of the former Bullocks Wilshire department store on Wilshire Boulevard into the law library of Southwestern University [14]. Bullocks Wilshire was a great Los Angeles institution, built in 1929–34 to designs by John & Donald Parkinson and heralding a decisive move of business away from the downtown area. The store finally closed in 1993 and was damaged a year later in the riots. Southwestern University's immaculate refurbishment, completed in 1997, has restored outstanding interiors containing some of the best American decorative art of the period, strongly influenced by French art deco.

If new architecture, the so-called 'heritage of the future', is vital to towns and cities, the rediscovery and reuse of old buildings and areas is even more significant in underpinning urban life in the twenty-first century. In many cases, the two work in partnership on one site – as with Ibos & Vitart's recasting of the Museum of Fine Arts in Lille (see pages 200–207). The contrast between old and new modernism is seen to particular effect in some of the industrial cities of northern England. During the 1960s and 1970s, usable old buildings were destroyed in favour of banal new developments which reflected a tragic loss of self-esteem – Bradford declined steadily in wealth and prestige after the Second World War. Now old buildings that have survived the carnage are being transformed. Few cities suffered worse than the old wool capital of Bradford, but the historic Gothic Revival Wool Exchange (Lockwood & Mawson, 1864–67) lingered on, its *raison d'être* long vanished but its fabric little changed. A rather unfortunate alteration of the 1890s, when part of the original, elaborate north façade was replaced by a plain stone elevation, opened the way for the transformation completed by architects Dempster, Thrussell & Rae in 1997. A slick new glazed frontage now offers views from the street into the main hall, well restored as a bookshop. Offices ring the hall – a relatively liberal planning approach allowed optimum use of the rather awkward spaces. The transformed building makes a bold statement about both conservation and the use of new materials in a historic context and forms a strong counterpoint to the severely Victorian character of the adjacent buildings. Ironically, it is the rarity value of buildings like the Wool Exchange, in the aftermath of post-1945 redevelopment, which has opened the way for imaginative reuse.

Terry Farrell, Tobacco Docks, London, 1989

John Outram, Judge Institute, Cambridge, 1995

The traumatic effects of economic and social change, leaving buildings, as well as people, dislocated and disconnected, were felt particularly strongly in the former East Germany after reunification. The city of Jena was dominated by the Carl Zeise optical works, employing 30,000 people out of a total population of around 100,000. The firm had to be radically restructured to survive in a competitive world – its main customer had been the Red Army – but its historic city-centre site was closed down, leaving a hole in the heart of Jena. The masterplan for regeneration drawn up by the British practice DEGW and implemented from 1992 onwards provided for the reuse of many of the buildings on the site (dating from c.1890 to 1960) for retail, office, hotel and educational use. A 140 metre- (459 foot-) long glazed galleria forms the new focus for the regenerated site.

The potential for reusing former industrial sites – and entire quarters – as contexts for a revival of life in the city is being realized particularly dramatically in Berlin. The success of the stylishly refurbished Hackesche Höfe (see pages 42–49) was, perhaps, entirely predictable, given the location and history of the site. The dramatic reconstruction of the former Osram factory (see pages 238–241) as an office and residential 'city within a city' was more risky, but is buoyed by the massive investment in Berlin as Germany's new capital. The strength of confidence in the city's future is underlined by the ongoing conversion of the former Schultheiss brewery at Kreuzberg, already one of the more agreeable residential quarters of Berlin, into loft-style apartments as part of a wholesale redevelopment of the site. Breweries had used the site since the 1860s: the Schultheiss brewery moved there in the 1890s, but has recently relocated to a new site in the former East Berlin. Given good transport connections, the vacant site offers obvious potential for residential use. The idea of a residential 'village' has been developed, with a strong emphasis on arts and cultural uses. Many of the existing buildings are protected monuments – only more recent structures can be cleared. One key feature is the huge, vaulted brewery undercroft which is envisaged as a potential new home for Berlin's State Museum of Modern Art, while other museum, gallery and studio uses will be actively encouraged. The project promises to be one of the key German transformation projects of the millennium.

ARCHITECTURE TRANSFORMED

Cities are about buildings, spaces and, above all, people. In *Space, Time and Architecture* (1941), a canonic text for architects and planners involved in post-war reconstruction, Sigfried Giedion insisted that 'the intricate disorder of the present day cannot continue'.[7] Yet it is this 'intricate disorder', central to the appeal of Venice, Barcelona and New York, which postmodern urbanists like Colin Rowe, Rob Krier and Aldo Rossi celebrated and which inspired Rem Koolhaas's *Delirious New York* (1978). The idea of a complete dissolution of the existing order has lost its appeal. When architects ceased to dream about a clean sweep of the past, a more pragmatic and humanistic postmodern architecture was born. Postmodern – but not necessarily postmodernist. Although the acceptance – indeed, the critical elevation – of ordinariness implicit in Robert Venturi's writings was another blow against a withered Modern culture, much postmodernist architecture, characterized by an opportunist pillaging of historic styles, seemed to some like a betrayal of history.[8] Indeed, postmodern urban projects like Quincy Market and Covent Garden were reiterated in many cities – in Baltimore, a new urban quarter, Harbor Place, was closely modelled on the Boston waterfront, but in this case the buildings were almost entirely new. At Tobacco Docks, in London's Docklands, Terry Farrell attempted a 'Covent Garden of the East End', a stylish reworking of old warehouses which was marred by the developer's insistence on overloading the site with pseudo-historical references, including reproduction sailing ships [15]. As David Harvey has pointed out, 'imaging a city through the organization of spectacular urban spaces became a means to attract capital and people (of the right sort) in a period (since 1973) of intensified urban competition and urban entrepreneurialism'.[9] Cynics began to talk about the emergence of a 'heritage industry'.[10]

A few architects of the postmodernist persuasion were capable of drawing inspiration from the past and applying it to current building types. James Stirling (who rejected the postmodernist label) was one; Michael Graves, at his best, another. The British architect John Outram has worked dramatic effects on a number of old buildings, most conspicuously perhaps at the former Addenbrookes Hospital in Cambridge, converted into Cambridge University's Judge Institute [16]. Outram is capable of transforming the ordinary into the exotic. A group of warehouses in Kent, recast in the 1980s into prestige offices from a very mundane existing building, exemplifies Outram's approach, which is about transformation in practical, aesthetic and symbolic terms. In this case, re-imaging the buildings was as much a priority – the new use demanded a new look – as updating their services.[11]

The best responses to historic buildings and towns have come from architects working in the modern tradition. 'I believe in conservation and in learning from history', declared Richard Rogers in 1990, conceding that Corbusier got it wrong, 'but merely copying the past belittles its integrity'.[12] Rogers'

Coop Himmelblau, Rooftop conversion, Vienna, 1988

Ron Herron, Imagination Building, London, 1989

transformation of the old Billingsgate Market in London (see pages 54–57) into a state-of-the-art dealing floor combined meticulous restoration and bold intervention. Relatively modest additions to historic buildings, such as the Sackler Galleries at London's Royal Academy, prefaced the major transformations by Norman Foster of the British Museum (pages 242–245) and of Berlin's Reichstag (pages 234–247). One school of transformation at the end of the twentieth century is founded on a disciplined and highly refined approach to the introduction of new elements which are sublimated to an overall aesthetic. The work of Herzog & de Meuron (pages 224–227), Yves Lion (pages 168–173) and, in Britain, Stanton Williams, is representative. (Stanton Williams' recent work includes immaculate refurbishments of the neoclassical Ashmolean Museum in Oxford and of London's National Theatre, a major work of the senior modern master Denys Lasdun.) Discipline and refinement do not preclude inventiveness. Stanton Williams' reconstruction of an Edwardian depository on London's Sloane Avenue represents an ideal balance of old and new, helped by a happy marriage of contrasting materials.

Another approach to transforming old buildings stresses contrast, dichotomy and even dissonance. The Viennese partnership Coop Himmelblau (Wolf Prix and Helmut Swiczinsky) expressed this mode perfectly in the now-famous rooftop extension completed in Vienna's Falkestrasse in 1988 [17]. The brief was to fit a new boardroom and offices on top of a nineteenth-century block in a historic thoroughfare. There was no attempt to defer to what existed, and the location helped in this respect. The new structure, 'a cross between a bridge and an aeroplane', as the architects describe it, is deliberately disruptive, but has a dynamic beauty of its own. Its lightweight engineering allows it to squat on the roof like a giant bird that might one day choose to take flight. Erick van Egeraat's work in central Budapest (pages 60–65) is in a similar vein of controlled fancy. Working for a Dutch developer, van Egeraat – whose refurbishment and extension of the Natural History Museum in Rotterdam (completed in 1996) prefigured the Hungarian projects – took as his raw material a dignified late nineteenth-century commercial palazzo on Andrassy Street. From the street, an immaculate restoration seems to have taken place; the drama happens at roof level, where a boardroom (nicknamed 'the whale') sits in space, glimpsed through a great cut made into the top of the old atrium. Budapest and Prague, great European cities little damaged by twentieth-century wars but long atrophied by Communism, have been receptive to the architecture of transformation. In Prague Castle, the Slovene architect Joze Plečnik brilliantly reworked an old symbol of Hapsburg domination as the powerhouse of a new democracy, too soon extinguished by

Nazi invasion. British architects Jestico & Whiles, working in Prague in the aftermath of the 'Velvet Revolution', had less exalted aims, yet their British Council offices and mixed-use refurbishment of the Ericsson Palace (see pages 68–71) express in architectural terms a new vision of a city that was for half a century full of closed doors, a city where beautiful façades often concealed physical (and political) decay.

Jestico & Whiles' approach to transformation, though pragmatic rather than purist, and concerned more with expressing the mechanics of architecture than the rhetoric of a style, has produced dramatic reworkings of old buildings in London (such as a furniture depository into studios and offices in Covent Garden and a drill hall into a record company headquarters in Chiswick) and Madrid. The British Council's new base in the Spanish capital is housed in a turn of the century mansion, long used as a school and virtually derelict when acquired. What was a highly compartmented building has been opened up for public use by the 'cone' cut through from first floor to roof levels and containing a lightweight metal stair. Jestico & Whiles describe their way of working as 'history-rooted' and 'non-dogmatic', which places them firmly within a British tradition of pragmatism. Yet there is an expressive element in the work which is found to even more striking effect in the Imagination Building in London, the major built work of the late Ron Herron, one of the founders of the Archigram group. The Imagination project – the transformation of a school into offices for a design and promotions company – was significant in raising the design profile of conversion schemes in Britain [18]. The use of a lightweight fabric roof to enclose the playground between the two wings of the school and turn it into a light-filled atrium helped accelerate the project (constructed between August 1988 and August 1989). Slender, vertiginous bridges criss-cross the atrium space to connect the two wings at all levels.

The fire that gutted part of Windsor Castle in 1992 aroused considerable interest in the potential for a creative reconstruction of the damaged interiors, notably the completely destroyed St George's Hall. The decision to commission a pallid historicist reconstruction confirmed many in their view that the Royal Family was no friend to innovative design. Yet the motive behind the rebuilding was to reassure, to cement together a failing institution, rather than to question or renew it. Meticulous reconstruction, achieved with the help of excellent craftsmanship, produced something entirely lifeless. Today, new and old overlap, mediate and confront each other fearlessly: deferring to the past is pointless.

Britain was the scene for some of the last great battles between clean-sweep modernism and the new architecture of urban accord. The greatest

Okada & Associates, Beer Museum, Sapporo, 1984

confrontation of the 1980s saw architects and critics, including Berthold Lubetkin, Richard Rogers and John Summerson, defending plans to demolish a block of Victorian commercial buildings in the City of London in order to create a site for a tower designed by Mies van der Rohe (long deceased) and a public square. Neither the Mies tower nor the conservationists' alternative strategy, a radical conversion scheme by Terry Farrell, was built. (The site is now occupied by a posthumous work of James Stirling.) But the debate over the site seemed to burn out the argument that keeping old buildings was somehow a retrogressive move.

The issue is no longer about new versus old, but about the nature of the vital relationship between the two. In European countries, the exact definition of the relationship is often a matter for intense debate between architects and historic buildings agencies such as English Heritage or the *Monuments Historiques*. But the recognition that existing buildings must be regarded as a scarce resource has spread far beyond Europe. Even in Japan, which has long combined a cult of modernity with an abstract veneration of history, nineteenth- and twentieth-century buildings are now being conserved and reused. Warehouses on the waterfront at Hakodate, Hokkaido have become shops, restaurants and conference facilities in a series of bold conversions by Okada & Associates (pages 174–177). A massive group of mill buildings in Kanazawa has re-emerged, after conversion by architect Ichiro Mizuno, as the Citizens' Art Centre (pages 142–145), opened in 1996 and housing concert halls, studios and galleries within the refurbished timber-framed interiors. At Sapporo, a city famous for its beer industry, a former brewery has been turned into a Beer Museum, with late nineteenth-century interiors sensitively adapted [19]. More curious, to Western sensibilities, is the Fish Paste Museum in Kanagawa which opened in 1996. The 1950s building is now open to visitors, who can experience 'hands on' the techniques formerly used to produce a staple of the Japanese diet. The increasing involvement of leading Japanese architects in refurbishment and extension projects – Yoshio Taniguchi, for example, is revamping New York's Museum of Modern Art – may reflect a maturing of Japanese architecture as well as a response to the mood of economic caution and retrenchment in Japan in the late 1990s.

Architectural conservation began with a concern to preserve monuments, but steadily moved on to a concern with urban form and the life it expressed – 'historical essence and continuous life' as Patrick Geddes described it. [13] André Malraux's *secteurs sauvegardes* inspired legislation in Britain and the USA in the 1960s designed to protect whole areas. The Modern Movement too was monument-obsessed and defiantly anti-history, but as a new modern architecture emerges, the old fetishes seem merely curious. The greatest challenge, indeed, for the twenty-first century is the legacy of the twentieth century. The new architecture is about process rather than product. It welcomes the dynamic of the future and addresses the lessons of the past. Above all, it celebrates diversity, recognizing the value of old and new, of modernity and tradition. In the words of David Chipperfield,

> We should not live in a bright shining new future, any more than we should hide in a comfortable pastiche of the past. We must inhabit an ever-evolving present, motivated by the possibilities of change, restricted by the baggage of memory and experience. [14]

That statement sums up the challenge of architectural transformation.

1. J. Jacobs, *Death and Life of Great American Cities*, New York 1961
2. J. Summerson, *Heavenly Mansions*, New York 1963, pp. 240–41
3. R. Cahan, *They All Fall Down: Richard Nickel's Struggle to Save America's Architecture*, Washington DC 1994
4. *Architecture Today*, 85, February 1998, p. 18
5. *Hans Döllgast, 1891–1974*, ed. Herausgeber Technische Universitat München, Bund Deutscher Architekten BDA, Munich 1987
6. C. Jencks, *Heteropolis: Los Angeles, the Riots and the Strange Beauty of Hetero-architecture*, London 1993
7. S. Giedion, *Space, Time and Architecture*, Cambridge, Mass. 1941, p. 545
8. R. Venturi, D. Scott Brown and S. Izenour, *Learning from Las Vegas*, Cambridge, Mass. 1972
9. D. Harvey, *The Condition of Post Modernity*, Oxford 1989, p. 92
10. R. Hewison, *The Heritage Industry*, London 1987
11. See *Architects' Journal*, 4 March, 1987, pp. 37–54
12. R. Rogers, *Architecture: A Modern View*, London 1990, p. 10
13. Quoted in S. Kostof, *The City Shaped*, London 1991, p. 86
14. *David Chipperfield: Recent Work*, Barcelona 1997, p. 131

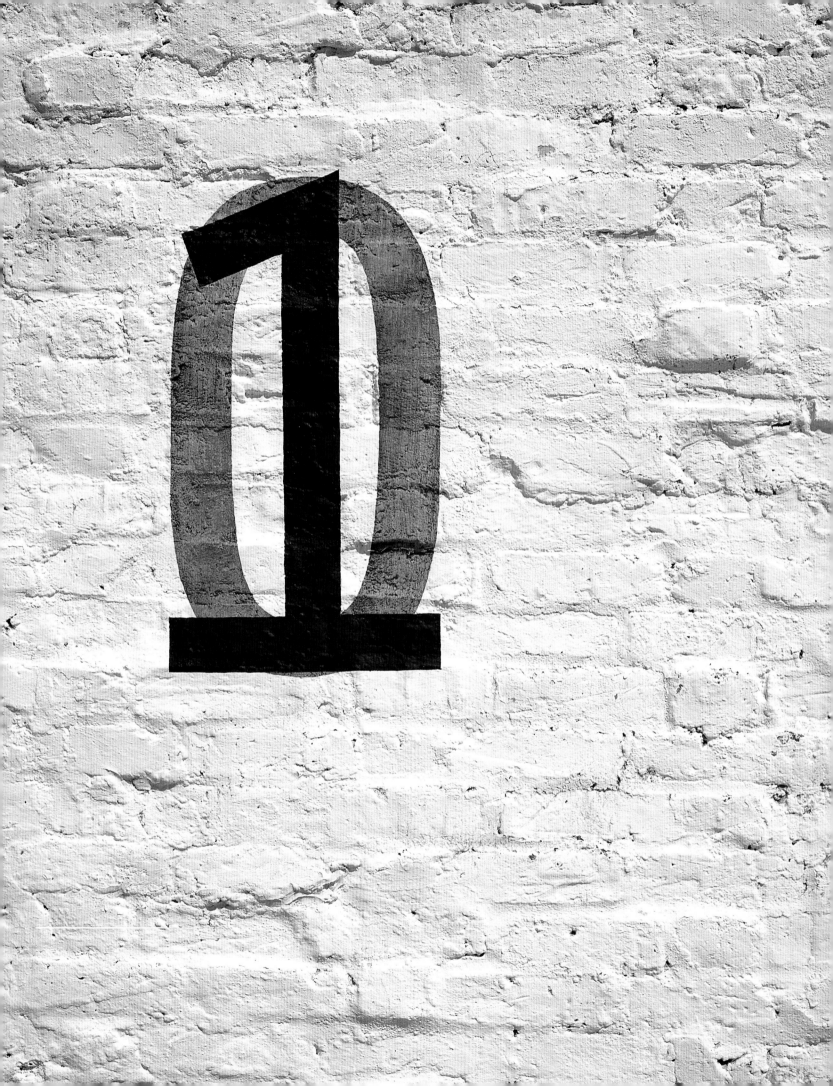

CHAPTER 1
LIVING & WORKING

Fifty years ago, in the aftermath of the Second World War, architects and planners in the developed world, cresting on a wave of popular opinion, set out to rebuild society. The model of America, whose cities were perceived as places of relentless change, was influential and the urban theories of Le Corbusier profoundly influenced a generation bent on radical change. The traditional city was seen as an anachronism and every old building as an affront. New housing was seen as the first priority. The late twentieth-century renaissance of cities, including those of the USA, has, in contrast, embraced the established urban scene, positively relishing the contrast between old and new. New landmarks like Frank Gehry's Bilbao Guggenheim, Jean Nouvel's Institut du Monde Arabe in Paris and Steven Holl's Kiasma Museum in Helsinki gain from their location in historic contexts. The new highlights the merits of the old, and both old and new are seen as vital elements in the life of a city.

The driving force behind the Modern Movement's agenda for reconstruction was a vision of a better life – healthier homes and more humane workplaces. The intentions were impeccable, but cloaked in utilitarian, even paternalistic, thinking which provided an easy target for critics of the modernist programme, who stressed the natural proclivity of humans to cling to the familiar and to value history and identity. In the twenty-first century, the ideal home and workplace will probably be located in a recycled building. The spiralling pace of economic change has provided the raw material for this revolution. The taste for living in converted factories and warehouses originated with artists, for purely practical reasons. The artists who colonized nineteenth-century New York warehouses in the 1960s pioneered the worldwide taste for 'lofts'. The loft has generated a lifestyle of its own and an aesthetic for living. Increasingly, developers have moved on from the relatively limited supply of old warehouses and mills, with their inbuilt resources of texture and structure, to more recent buildings, including post-1945 commercial buildings rendered obsolete by their inability to accommodate new information technology. It seems certain that this process will affect similar structures worldwide – Tokyo, for example, has many buildings of the 1950s and 1960s that could adapt to residential use, were the imperative to demolish and redevelop removed. The slowing down of the Far Eastern economies may be the spur that is needed to promote a process of transformation and reuse, rather than destruction.

The modern workplace – the office block – has been a prime generator of twentieth-century architecture. Frank Lloyd Wright's Larkin Building and Johnson Wax offices, Mies van der Rohe's Seagram Building and Richard Rogers' Lloyd's of London are icons in architectural history. The demands of information

technology underpinned a new generation of office buildings in the 1980s, when raised floors and open dealing rooms were key features of major projects such as New York's World Financial Center and London's Canary Wharf and Broadgate. The New York architectural practice Kohn Pedersen Fox (KPF) came to London in the late 1980s to work on Canary Wharf and other schemes. KPF chose to locate, however, not in a new building but in a refurbished warehouse in Covent Garden. Just as artists pioneered the contemporary taste for 'loft living', architects and designers – including Frank Gehry, Richard Meier and Richard Rogers – have tended to eschew new buildings in favour of transformed industrial and commercial spaces. Their example has been taken up by business operations generally. According to Frank Duffy, 'the office tower may soon be as redundant as the steam-powered mill... Instead, creative office work will be devolved to any location – a converted warehouse in a city centre, a kitchen in a country cottage, another country...' [1] Duffy's ideal model for the office of the future, the interactive 'club', functions ideally in a converted old building with generous spaces and a high degree of adaptability. The workplace of the future is about ideas and interaction, rather than repetitive drudgery – the computer has made the ledger book and the filing cabinet obsolete.

The office revolution is breaking down the divide between home and workplace – for many people, the same spaces double up as both. For the city, the implications are enormous. Old-style modernist planning rigorously segregated industrial, business and residential quarters, initiating suburbs that were lifeless by day and city centres that were empty at night. A recycled building may now contain new-style industry, offices and apartments within the same city block. Modern Movement planning destroyed cities. Today cities are being reassembled as the tyranny of zoning is overthrown. Entire areas of cities, abandoned as commercially moribund, are being recolonized as the nurseries of new industries and a new way of life.

1. F. Duffy, *The New Office*, London 1997, p. 97

THE LINGOTTO TURIN, ITALY

RENZO PIANO BUILDING WORKSHOP, 1988–1997

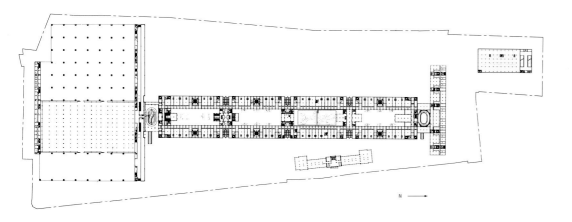

facing page: The former Fiat Lingotto factory was one of Europe's largest industrial buildings when completed in 1923. Its exterior has been little changed in the massive refurbishment by Renzo Piano.

above: First-floor plan. This main public level features landscaped courtyards with cafés and a shopping centre.

following page: The former rooftop test track with its glazed conference room.

The transformation of the Lingotto, the vast and legendary Fiat factory in Turin, into a multi-use, cultural and commercial complex – a true 'city within the city' – is one of the most heroic achievements in the field of architectural transformation to date.

The factory was built in 1917–23 and was big even by North American standards – the automated Ford plants in Detroit inspired the designs by engineer G. M. Trucco. The five-storey structure was a third of a mile long and provided for a vertical production line. Raw materials came in at the ground floor. Finished cars were tested on the rooftop track, a symbol of modernism that was used by Le Corbusier in *Vers une architecture* (1923). A number of ancillary buildings, including an office block (the *palazzina*), were added around the main block over the years. The Lingotto was the industrial heart of Italy: 12,000 people worked there. Fiat began, however, to devolve its operations to new sites during the 1950s. In 1982 the last car came off the Lingotto's production line, which had been made obsolete by automation and new working methods.

The demolition of the factory was never envisaged, however. An invited competition to find a conversion strategy was organized by Fiat in 1983–84 but it was not until 1986 that Piano (who had proposed a mixed-use, phased development) was asked to progress the project.

Planning discussions extended over a further two years as a development corporation was brought into being, with Fiat as a component. Work on site started in 1988. The approach of Piano and his colleagues was to respect the concrete-framed structure – 'if you try anything extravagant, you might kill the building', was Piano's view – but not to revere it. The basic discipline of the building and its grid were accepted, but many elements – for example, all the windows – were replaced. Given the scale of the existing factory (over 0.23 million square metres, 2.5 million square feet), the decision to build a new 46,000 square-metre (500,000 square-foot) exhibition hall next to it might seem over-ambitious. But the space needed for big trade fairs could not be entirely housed within the old buildings and the success of the trade fair operation (37 shows took place during 1997) has been a catalyst for the success of the hotel (opened in 1994) and office developments within the factory itself. The magnificent, 2,000-seat concert/conference hall is another new element, buried beneath a courtyard.

One of the problems faced by the architects was the uncertainty over the development's future occupants. Turin University, for example, once planned to occupy space, but later withdrew. A multiplex cinema is now set to take up the vacant area. The tough character of the factory allowed for a high degree of adaptability and the architects have been anxious not to compromise this quality. With the site steadily filling up – over 185,000 square metres (2 million square feet) of space was occupied by early 1997 – and a further boost provided by Fiat's decision to reoccupy the *palazzina* offices, the Lingotto project appears to have succeeded.

Many of the interventions made are anything but preservationist. Some of the original buildings have been cleared to give the development a spacious setting, including parkland to the west and a great piazza to the east, facing the city centre. Piano's now-celebrated 'bubble' structure, completed in 1996, containing a rooftop conference suite linked to a heli-pad, is an unashamedly fanciful and extrovert gesture. But it has given the Lingotto a new image for the future. Once associated with a heroic industrial past, the site is now clearly part of the future of Turin.

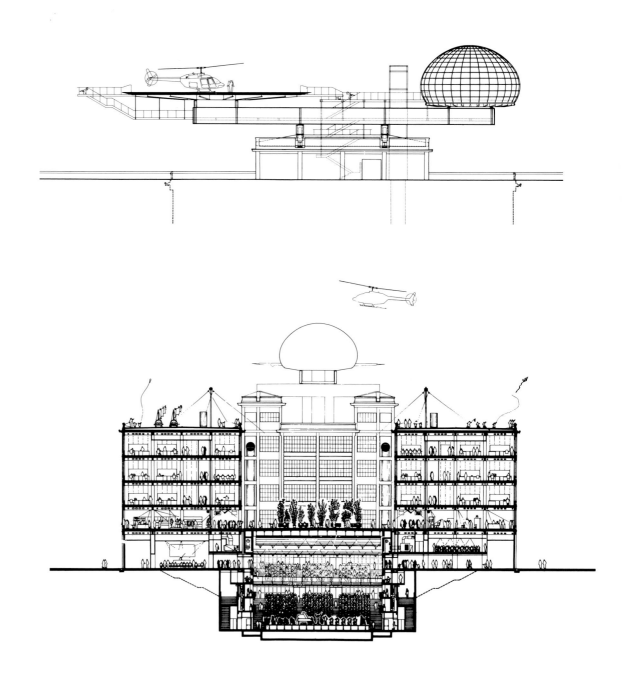

top: A dramatic feature of the conversion scheme is the construction of a new conference
room, counterbalanced by a heli-pad, at roof level.
above: Section through the converted building showing the large auditorium at basement level.
facing page: The smallest conference room, supported by an immense beam,
is clad in curved sheets of reflective double glazing. Motorized blinds have been fitted to those
parts receiving the most direct sunlight.

The multi-purpose cherry panelled conference/concert hall seats 2,000 people and is a key
element in the new life of the Lingotto. An adjustable ceiling varies the volume and acoustics.

Cross-section showing the concert hall.

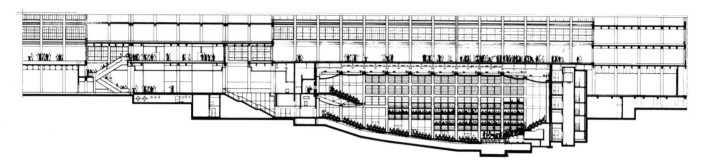

GRAVES HOUSE PRINCETON, NEW JERSEY, USA

MICHAEL GRAVES ARCHITECT, 1974–93

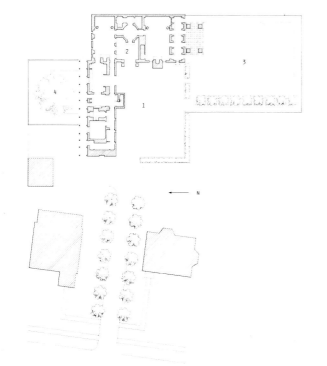

Site plan

1 Forecourt
2 Courtyard

3 East garden
4 West garden

facing page: Michael Graves's house at Princeton, formerly a furniture depository, is externally discreet and restrained, reflecting the character of a simple industrial building.

It is unusual for a relatively small project to occupy the attention of a world architect for two decades, but architects' own houses tend to be long-running jobs. The 'Warehouse' (as Michael Graves calls it) took nearly 20 years to bring to completion: it is one of the most interesting of Graves's projects. It was, indeed, a warehouse, completed in 1926 in the midst of a quiet residential enclave in the East Coast university town of Princeton. Students there had to leave their rooms during the vacation, and academics went off on study tours, sometimes for a year. The warehouse was run as a depository, where possessions could be stored: everything from a crate of books to a grand piano or the entire contents of a house. Inside were 44 cell-like rooms, which could be rented. The building, it was said, had been constructed by Italian masons moonlighting from their work on new university buildings, and it certainly had a rustic Italian look, complete with stucco render and clay-tile roof.

Graves, a member of the faculty at Princeton, bought the building in 1970, after the depository operation had closed down. Planning problems delayed any start on conversion, which began on site only in 1974. It took three years before the building was habitable – there were no services, apart from one cold-water tap – and even then only one wing of the L-shaped structure was lived in, the remainder being left as a shell. The west wing, the first part to be occupied, was renovated after the completion of the larger north wing in 1987. Only in 1992 was the entire scheme completed, with landscaping works finished the following year.

Graves's approach to the conversion reflected his passionate interest in classicism, the influence of which has predominated in his work from the mid-1970s. Graves greatly admires the work of John Soane and concedes that the latter's house in London was a significant source. Like all classicists, Graves is enamoured of Italy and looked to the modest but dignified farmhouses of the Italian countryside for inspiration. Comfort, rather than ostentation, was the aim in shaping his own home. The exterior of the house was left comparatively unadorned, a foil to the highly architectural garden layout. Inside, the basic structure was generally retained, so that the rooms have low ceilings and none is over-large, though the plan was greatly rationalized. The house is seen as a series of linked volumes, with no grand gestures. The only double-height spaces are the kitchen and the library (which terminates the north wing and can be looked into from the first-floor master bedroom). Entering the house via the *cortile* – once a loading bay for removal trucks – the visitor encounters a clearly rhetorical gesture in the form of an open oculus to the first floor and the skylit dome above. This is an obvious quotation from Soane. Elsewhere, the rhetoric is restrained. Natural light was a priority throughout: controlling daylight, Graves believes, is at the heart of good architecture. Windows are of steel, of an entirely modern pattern, but mixed in size and located to provide variable lighting conditions. Views out to the garden are carefully managed – the house stands, in fact, in a relatively small island of land, hemmed in by other houses.

An important consideration in the design of the Graves House was its role as a repository for Michael Graves's collections of furniture, works of art and books. The design of the individual rooms is calculated to display artefacts to best effect, without sacrificing normal standards of domestic comfort. Architectural and decorative devices, such as non-structural columns, are used as required, purely for effect. Functionalism is not an issue in Graves's architecture. The house could be seen as a postmodernist monument, but it is really a more personal achievement and Graves's plan is to see it preserved as a museum or study centre. It deserves attention as a unique, non-modernist example of architectural transformation.

left: Graves's library is formed within a double-height space at the end of one of the wings.

right: The internal proportions of the house are determined by the structure of the existing building, but the spaces have been dramatized by the introduction of columns and other architectural devices.

facing page: Above the entrance hall, a circular opening admits light from a new cupola – a device that recalls the work of John Soane.

Section through the entrance wing, showing the double-height library space.

RETAIL AND OFFICE DEVELOPMENT INNSBRUCK, AUSTRIA

PETER LORENZ, 1990–92

facing page: The historic Alt-Insprugg has been extended to the rear in a straightforward contemporary manner.

Peter Lorenz, one of the leaders of the remarkable renaissance of Austrian architecture of recent years, insists that working in the context of the past is an essential element in the diverse and broad-minded approach toward architecture in the late twentieth century. According to Lorenz, a reassuringly familiar past can conceal an 'embryonic smugness... [and] a well-protected romanticism', where 'prejudice safeguards from analysis, reflection and recognition'.

Innsbruck, where Lorenz practises architecture, is a picturesque historic town in the Tyrol. But its prettiness cannot hide some grim chapters of history – such as the enthusiasm of many locals in the 1930s for Nazism. The historic structure, the Alt-Insprugg, that formed the raw material for this transformational scheme was, in fact, the headquarters of the Nazi youth movement after the *Anschluss* in 1938. The Alt-Insprugg dates from the fifteenth century, but had been fitted for its sinister role by an early twentieth-century renovation which, though superficially picturesque with its evocation of Austrian and German mythology, anticipated the darker fantasies of the Hitlerite regime.

The transformation of this landmark building into modern shops, showrooms and offices therefore had to confront ideological as well as practical issues. Whatever its history, the building enjoyed protected status and its street frontage could not be altered. Existing interiors had to be restored as found. The rear elevation, where later extensions were removed, was rebuilt in a very simple manner. In extending the building, however, Lorenz was able to provide the most

dramatic contrast possible to its claustrophobic historicism. The key move was the cutting of a passage, sinking below street level, to link the new extension to the street and integrate it with the old building. The new structure, replacing derelict buildings of no historic interest, sits between the party walls of adjacent buildings, a beautifully detailed glazed box that eschews historical references. At the rear, there is a sleek new elevation and fine views out over the mountains. Between old and new, there is a glazed courtyard, its roof supported by slender trusses. (Such a space in northern Europe is potentially rather gloomy for much of the year, but the ingenious use of large swivelling mirrors provides natural light on the darkest days.) The old and new buildings are linked by cable-braced upper-level walkways, floored with timber slats, which have a symbolic as well as a practical role. (There is also a glazed lift for access to upper floors, a miracle of minimalist engineering.) The new building was designed to work in combination with the refurbished upper floors of the old structure, the whole space being let to a bank.

The commercial success of the scheme is obvious: a back land has been brought into relatively intensive use. The skill with which this objective has been achieved is not in dispute. For the architect, however, the success of the scheme lies as much in the way it has challenged an insular and protective view of society, as expressed in its buildings. The Alt-Insprugg has been both preserved and transformed.

Old building   New building

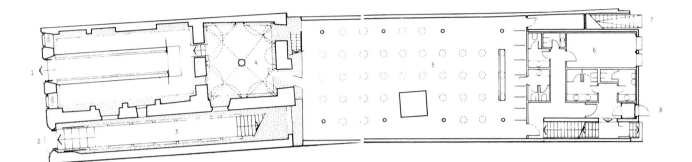

Semi-basement

1   Street entrance   5   Showroom
2   Entrance to shops   6   Café/kitchen
3   Passage through the old buildings 7   Service entrance
4   Showroom under Gothic vaults   8   West entrance ramps

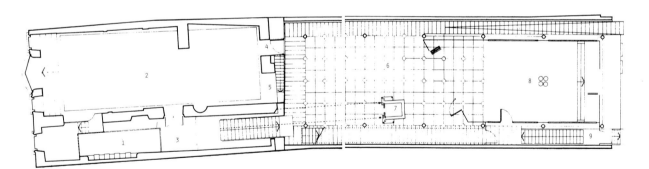

Mezzanine

1   Passage below
2   Showroom in the neo-Baroque hall   6   Glass-covered courtyard
3   Gallery   7   Glass lift
4   Entrance to showroom   8   Café/bar
5   Showroom display   9   Staircase from semi-basement

facing page: A sunken passageway connects the new extension with the street, without compromising the retained historic building.
following page: A lightweight glazed roof covers the open court between old and new buildings, providing a benign meeting and circulation space.

THE HACKESCHE HÖFE BERLIN, GERMANY

WEISS & FAUST, 1993-97

facing page: The largely destroyed frontage to the Rosenthaler Strasse has been reconstructed as a reinterpretation, rather than a replica, of what previously existed.

For nearly half a century, Berlin was divided by the physical barrier of the Wall, and became a city without an obvious heart. The open city of the West focused on the affluent but rather characterless Kurfürstendamm, while the historic centre – Berlin Mitte – with its great public monuments, was sunk in the East. With reunification, the life of Berlin has moved eastwards again, colonizing buildings and whole areas atrophied by the years of Communism. The success of the Hackesche Höfe project reflects both a degree of nostalgia amongst Berliners for the lifestyle that existed before the Second World War and equally a forward-looking commitment to mixed-use, high density urban development. In its way, the Hackesche Höfe scheme is as vital to Berlin as the rebuilt Potsdamer Platz.

The *höfe*, or courtyards, off the Hackeschen Markt, close to Museum Island, were the result of a comprehensive development project of the 1900s which included apartments, shops, offices and restaurants – around 26,000 square metres (279,861 square feet) of space in total. The overall design of the complex was the work of the Berlin architect Kurt Berndt, but August Endell (1871–1925), who had worked for a time in Munich and been strongly influenced by *Jugendstil* art, was responsible for some of the façades and internal decor. Damaged in the Second World War, the Hackesche Höfe might well have been cleared under DDR planning policies, but somehow survived, a haven, in particular, for small businesses. Though physically dilapidated and partly derelict, the Hackesche Höfe generated a strong spirit of community – which was reinforced by the artists and small entrepreneurs who moved in after the fall of the Wall – and a powerful sense of place. (Wim Wenders filmed part of his remarkable *Wings of Desire* in the Hackesche Höfe.) The regeneration of the area involved a collaboration between the existing community and the new investors. The

residents of the 80 apartments largely stayed put, benefiting from the refurbishment of the apartments and from the relocation of car repair firms and other small manufacturing enterprises, which made way for shops, studios and art galleries. The Hackesche Höfe quickly became a prime destination for tourists, while office spaces were snapped up by architects and designers.

Straightforward repair and restoration formed a major part of the project. The once elaborate frontage to the Rosenthaler Strasse had been meanly rebuilt in the 1960s. There was much debate about its restoration: the design (by Bernhard Leisering) that was eventually executed is a spirited reinterpretation of the original, rather than a replica, and avoids the coarseness of much recent postmodern commercial architecture in Berlin. Behind, Endell's elaborately tiled courtyard façades have been painstakingly restored and the best of his interiors, including a restaurant, a staircase and ballrooms, have also been reinstated. Now, as in the 1900s, this yard (the so-called *Jugendstilhof*) contains restaurants and bars and is regularly packed with visitors. The other yards are less flamboyant and progressively less frequented as shops and offices give way to residential blocks, the latter externally clad in plain render. The hard landscape of the more public spaces is softened in the residential areas of the Spielhof and Brunnenhof by generous planting. Some apartments look out over the adjacent burial ground of the Sophienkirche and the former Jewish Cemetery.

The entire project was closely monitored by the city's historic buildings inspectorate, but there was an implicit acceptance that, the restored Endell interiors apart, internal reconstruction could be radically new – hence the strikingly contemporary character of, for example, Ben Van Berkel's Aedes Gallery, a prime venue for architectural exhibitions.

above: The innermost courts of the Hackesche Höfe are largely residential
in character, as they have always been.
facing page: Ben Van Berkel's Aedes Gallery.

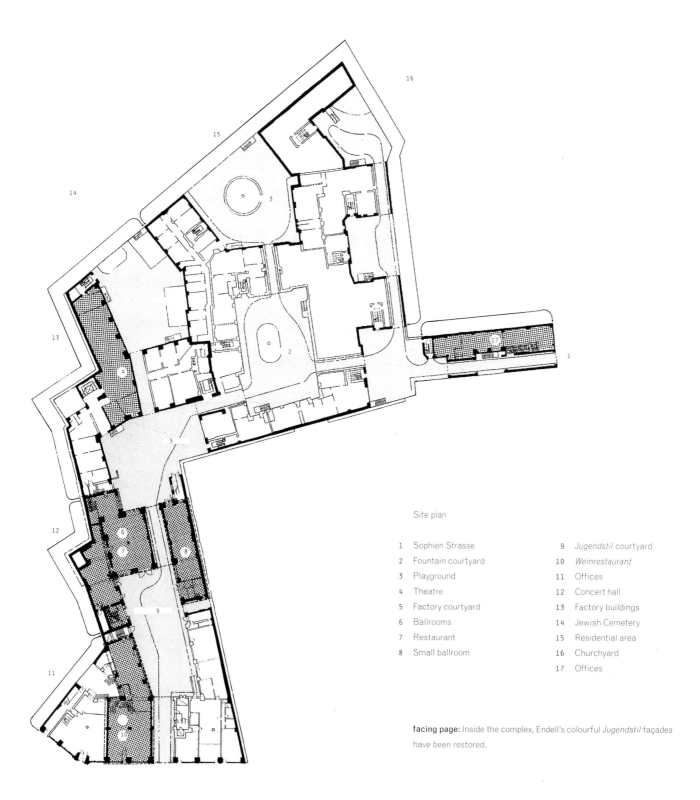

Site plan

1	Sophien Strasse	9	*Jugendstil* courtyard
2	Fountain courtyard	10	*Weinrestaurant*
3	Playground	11	Offices
4	Theatre	12	Concert hall
5	Factory courtyard	13	Factory buildings
6	Ballrooms	14	Jewish Cemetery
7	Restaurant	15	Residential area
8	Small ballroom	16	Churchyard
		17	Offices

facing page: Inside the complex, Endell's colourful *Jugendstil* façades have been restored.

above: The studio of architects Diener & Diener.
facing page: The Chameleon variety club, with internal decor by Endell.

MARIO BELLINI STUDIO MILAN, ITALY

MARIO BELLINI ASSOCIATI, 1990-93

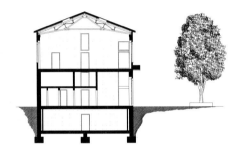

facing page: Ground-floor hall with reception area. The hall cuts across the whole building and is marked off by metal columns that culminate with a skylight.

left: Section: the existing structure has been largely retained.

right: The courtyard has been restored, following the introduction of underground parking space; external additions remain unobtrusive.

Mario Bellini is, perhaps, better known outside Italy as a product designer than as an architect, but his architectural projects – such as the extensions to the Milan Fiera – include large-scale new buildings in a broadly postmodernist tradition. Bellini's own offices, however, are located in a converted building in an old industrial quarter of Milan – chosen both for its good value and because it offered Bellini the scope for an imaginative conversion.

The old foundry in Milan's Piazza Arcole was semi-derelict when identified as a possible new workspace for Bellini and three other architectural practices. The complex was a renovated space, ranged around three sides of a quadrangle. Each practice carried out internal work to its own designs while Bellini was responsible for the exteriors and landscape. The Bellini offices take up one side of the square. This 1,600 square metres (17,222 square feet) of space is around a third of the site's total area.

The buildings were structurally sound and needed only redecoration, new services and repairs to the roofs and windows. However, a major element in the project was the provision of subterranean parking below the central courtyard. Mario Bellini believes that architects should work from relatively basic premises: the architect is a mobile professional, moving from site to site, he says. Architectural offices should not be dominated by technology, rooting architects to the spot – 'historically speaking, an architect's office has been a mobile office'.

Though long-abandoned, the foundry buildings had been scheduled as of historic interest, so any major alterations were ruled out. Bellini had no quarrel with this: reuse is an old Italian tradition, he says. The restored ochre stucco on the buildings' façades looks timeless. External additions such as door hoods and trellises for plants are minor and unobtrusive. Inside Bellini's own studio, the main space (the drawing office) is at first-floor level and open to the steel roof structure (where ventilation ducts are freely exposed). The building is entered at the centre, where a new construction sits squarely within the space. It is a brutally industrial artefact, constructed of steel columns and perforated steel flooring, and gives access to the upper floors by means of stairs and a lift. The intention is to contrast the regular machine-made interventions with the simply rendered walls. Steel galleries form a strong grid at the centre of the studio.

The Bellini studio provides a very clear statement of the designer's credo – the contrast between the sheer ordinariness of the old building and the stylish additions is typically Italian. But it is also a pragmatic reworking of a solid structure which, originally used to form ironwork, now produces ideas and drawings.

facing page: The Bellini studio is a lofty, naturally lit space –
its existing industrial ethos has been preserved.

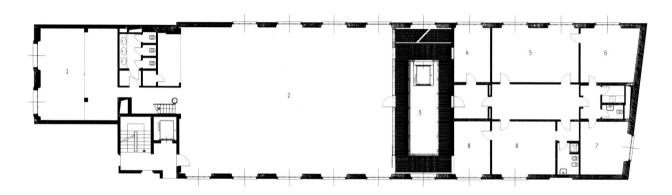

First floor

1 Store room   5 Meeting room
2 Drawing office: 6 Archive
   architectural division   7 Office
3 Entrance hall   8 Studios
4 Secretary's office

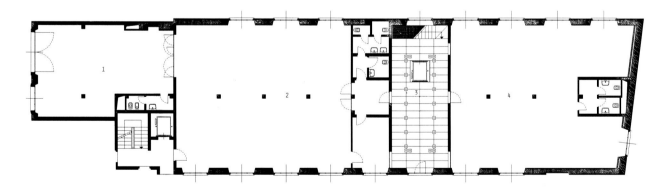

Ground floor

1 Workshop   3 Entrance hall
2 Drawing office: 4 Open space
   industrial division

BILLINGSGATE MARKET CONVERSION LONDON, UK

RICHARD ROGERS PARTNERSHIP, 1985–88

left: A frameless wall of glass set behind the classical street elevation, with its elegant
iron gates, provides natural light and a visual connection to the outside world.
right: Great care has been taken with the detailing of the glazed screen to ensure
maximum transparency and lightness.

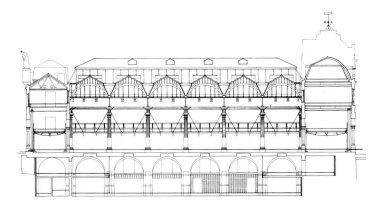

Section through the converted Billingsgate market: additional space has been provided in suspended mezzanine floors.

The conversion of the City of London's redundant wholesale fish market, that had occupied the site since Saxon times, into state-of-the-art dealing floor space, by a leading world practice not hitherto associated with rehabilitation work, was a landmark in the history of building transformation.

Billingsgate had become a campaigning cause for British conservationists in the early 1980s. The City Corporation had built a new market in the Docklands and decided to sell the old building for demolition and redevelopment with offices. Constructed between 1874–77 under corporation architect Horace Jones, the market combined an elaborately decorated exterior – in deference to its location close to the Tower of London and Tower Bridge (the latter also designed by Jones) – with an essentially functional, but highly elegant interior of iron and glass. The conservation lobby demanded that the building be retained and asked the government to list it, a move strongly opposed by the City.

An outline scheme by Chrysalis Architects, commissioned by SAVE Britain's Heritage, demonstrated the practicality of reuse, with new offices on an adjacent parking lot. The building was subsequently listed. Since demolition had effectively been ruled out, the City looked for a buyer. Citibank, a major American bank seeking electronic dealing floor space in London, acquired the market, seeing its open floor space as ideal for their requirements.

The Victorian market consisted of a ground-floor trading area (surrounded by cellular offices on three sides and open to an impressive timber, iron and glass roof); a gallery (the Haddock Gallery) extending above this principal space at second-floor level in a north–south direction; and a brick-vaulted basement supporting the superstructure and itself resting on a 3 metre- (33 foot-) thick concrete floor slab. The retention of the main internal space, (a condition of planning consent for conversion), was entirely compatible with the needs of the new users. A massive upgrading of services was, however, required to support both a permanent workforce of over 500 and a large amount of electronic equipment.

Billingsgate had suffered from years of neglect and under-maintenance. Many original features had been lost and others had deteriorated badly. The timber roof structure needed a major overhaul, with the replacement of rotten parts. Lead coverings were replaced in the traditional manner. Externally, the market was faithfully restored to its 1877 state and the cleaning of its eclectic neo-Renaissance façades revealed qualities that had been largely ignored. Inside, the approach was to combine restoration with new interventions. Lighting was a fundamental issue, both aesthetically and functionally. Conventional glass in the main roof and that of the Haddock Gallery was replaced by prismatic glazing units which excluded direct sunlight and glare and filtered in a steady north light. A frameless, glazed wall – using 25mm- (1 inch-) thick glass to ensure soundproofing – was set back beyond the street elevation and provided further natural light and a sense of contact with the outside world. Artificial lighting for the new dealing floor was provided using fluorescent linear up- and down-lights, supplying ideal conditions for screenwork which also highlighted the historic structure.

The major intervention into the old building was the construction of a mezzanine floor of lightweight reinforced concrete, suspended from the Haddock Gallery, to provide extra accommodation. The floor of the Haddock Gallery itself was structurally reinforced to permit heavier loads. New floors were introduced into the perimeter wings, reused as cellular management offices and meeting rooms. A reinforced concrete floor-slab, 250mm (10 inches) thick, was laid over the brick vaults to transfer loads from the new superstructure to the existing substructure.

At basement level, extensive alterations – including the addition of intermediate floors across part of the space – provided for the insertion of services. Full air-conditioning was installed, with air-handling on the main floor level conducted through a raised floor into specially designed perimeter units. The high servicing requirements of the refurbished building necessitated the construction of an additional plant room under the river bank for water storage tanks.

Richard Rogers' masterly Lloyd's Building was completed while the Billingsgate project was under way. Lloyd's was essentially a modern market hall. At Billingsgate, Rogers housed late twentieth-century market traders (dealing in shares rather than fish) in an old market hall, providing an essential continuity of use while giving the listed building an assured future life. The scheme challenged preconceptions, then widespread in Britain, that new work in a historic building must be 'in keeping' with surrounding buildings. Rogers' radical approach maintained a clear distinction between old and new work and the elegance of the latter demonstrated respect for the dignity of the existing fabric. The project won a number of awards and was even praised by the Prince of Wales, whose campaigns of the 1980s were directed against modernism of the Rogers school. Although never, in the event, used by Citibank, Billingsgate was subsequently acquired by another financial institution, which found it ideal for its needs.

above: The interior space has remained uncompromised in the conversion to dealing space.

facing page: The former Haddock Gallery has been reused as a trading space, with its floor reinforced.

HOUSE EXTENSION BUDERIM, QUEENSLAND, AUSTRALIA

CLARE DESIGN, 1995

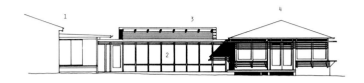

North elevation

1   Existing house and verandah
2   Gallery

3   Skylight to bathroom and wardrobe
4   Garage converted to bedroom

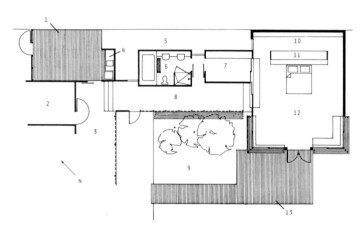

Ground-floor plan

facing page: Lindsay and Kerry Clare's conversion of a former garage has provided not just a bedroom, but a place in which to relax and even work, much extending the life of the house to which it is attached.

1   Deck
2   Existing house
3   Existing verandah
4   Laundry
5   Landscaping
6   Bathroom
7   Wardrobe

8   Gallery
9   Northern courtyard
10 Studio
11 Desk
12 Bedroom
13 Deck

Lindsay and Kerry Clare, the partners in Clare Design, are enthusiasts for the vernacular buildings of Queensland and their architecture falls firmly within a 'regionalist' mould. Their work, however, draws inspiration from a wider modern tradition – notably that stemming from Scandinavia – and reflects the late twentieth-century concern with issues of environment and ecology. They seek an appropriate modern architecture for a tropical climate, where outdoor living has long been the custom and where – to quote Glenn Murcutt, another Australian architect – buildings traditionally 'touch the ground lightly'.

The house extension at Buderim, Queensland, is a conversion of an existing double garage. The owners, who had lived in the house for several years before commissioning the extension, recognized the irony of an arrangement where living and sleeping space was in short supply, while cars were housed in comfort. Typical of conventional Queensland houses of its era, the existing home had very small bedrooms. The Clares' project therefore transformed the garage – a basic concrete-block structure – into a new master bedroom, linked to the existing house by an open passage. (In this region of Australia, rain falls on average only twice a year!) The new dressing room and bathroom are located off this passage, which also serves as a showplace for a collection of art objects.

The transformed space is, in fact, much more than a bedroom. It is a place to relax and, on occasion, to work. Casement windows can be opened on to a new deck facing the pool and garden, where there is ample space to sit and enjoy the view. Equally, however, there is a workstation built into the bed's headboard, which demarcates a small study area for quiet work away from the family. The aesthetics of the conversion are determinedly minimal – creating a look of restraint suitable for the hot climate.

59

ING AND NNH BANK BUDAPEST, HUNGARY

ERICK VAN EGERAAT ASSOCIATED ARCHITECTS, 1992–97

facing page: Erick van Egeraat's refurbishment of the original 1880s block culminates in a conference room, nicknamed 'the whale', sitting on top of the courtyard.

Erick van Egeraat's project for the ING and NNH Bank was executed in two phases, one primarily a refurbishment of an existing building, the other an entirely new, 5,000 square-metre (53,819 square-foot) extension to the same building. The two phases merge, however, as a subtle yet dramatic fusion of old and new. It is, in Egeraat's own description, a 'juxtaposition of an uncompromising modernism with intuitive organic shapes to achieve what might be called a "modern baroque"'.

The original bank building, completed in 1882, faces on to Andrassy Street. It is an imposing essay in the eclectic historicism of its age, and is now protected as a building of historic interest. The focus of the 1880s block was the central courtyard, although this was never a functional space. In 1992–94 the building was completely refurbished, with faithful restoration of period features. The so-called 'whale', a conference room of distinctly 'organic' form which now sits on top of the courtyard (sealed as an interior space) is, however, a bold addition and is a stunningly sculptural object in its own right. Above the old building there is a new domain of steel and glass, where the 'whale' can be read as a three-dimensional object.

The extension of the bank on to Paulay Ede Street, completed in 1997, makes no attempt to echo the architecture of the existing building. It is entirely clad in glass, aluminium-framed, the façade tilted slightly out of the vertical to avoid reflections and sunk directly into the pavement at street level, without any kind of base. This is a climatic façade, double-glazed and incorporating a return air system. Where the new elevation meets the 1880s façade, it is imprinted with an image, in fritted glass, of the old frontage, an elusive presence which can be seen clearly from an angle at a distance, but vanishes when seen face on at close range. Is this respect for history – or an ironic commentary on transience?

There is no structural division between the two buildings. Floor levels run through into the new extension from those in the 1880s block – the all-glass façades are helpful in lighting a deep-section building. The staircase is a *tour de force*, suspended from a system of steel cables and supplemented by transparent lifts.

Erick van Egeraat is an acknowledged master of the new glass architecture and adept at making all-glass façades respond to new imperatives on ecology and user-comfort. The Budapest scheme shows how a preoccupation with innovative materials and technology can be combined with the transformation of a historic fabric to form a new whole which is well suited to present-day needs. Few recent projects achieve the radical dichotomy and balance of this one.

left: Egeraat's extension, completed in 1997, makes no attempt at pastiche but is a strikingly innovative exercise in glazing techniques.
right: The new conference room is connected by a dramatic stair to the upper level of the courtyard.

left: The conference room is invisible from street level, but enlivens the city's skyline.

right: The connection between old and new work is uncompromising in its directness.

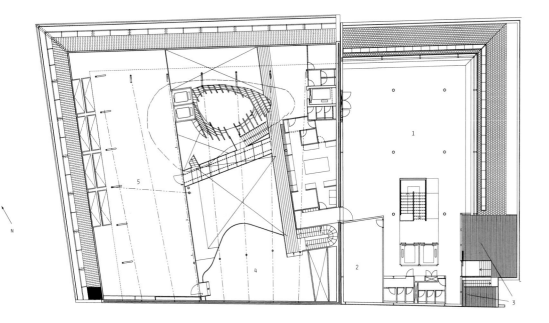

Attic mezzanine

1 Lunchroom
2 Coffee corner
3 Kitchen
4 Open-plan office
5 Roof terrace

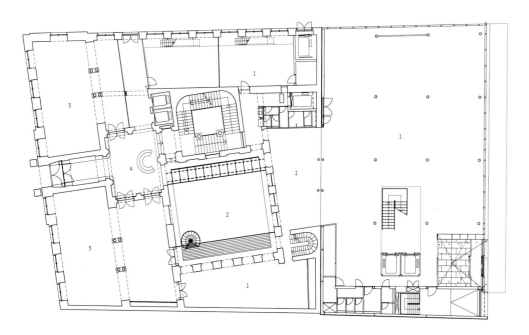

Ground floor

1 Office
2 Courtyard
3 Banking hall
4 Reception

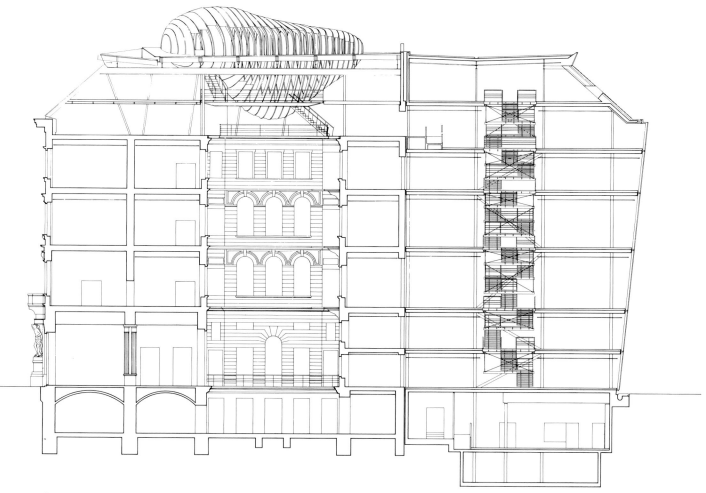

MEWS HOUSE EDINBURGH, SCOTLAND

RICHARD MURPHY ARCHITECTS, 1994–95

facing page, left: View from the living room to the bedroom. The cantilevered wardrobe has a door that slides open to screen off the two rooms.
facing page, right: The conversion expresses the idea of a new home inserted into the repaired shell of an existing coach house.

Richard Murphy's considerable reputation has been forged almost entirely on the basis of projects for the conversion and extension of existing buildings. These include a number of additions to houses in Edinburgh, where he has his office. The transformation of a former coach house in Royal Terrace Mews, dating from the 1840s, reflects the continuing influence on Murphy of Carlo Scarpa, the subject of extensive research by the architect – evidence of the recent revival of interest in Britain in Scarpa's work.

The raw material for the scheme was a coach house, accommodating carriage and horses at mews level, with space for storing hay above. (A tiny sleeping cabin for a stable boy would probably also have been provided.) Some decades ago, the ground floor was radically altered for use as a garage, and the first-floor space became redundant. At this point, a crude concrete lintel was substituted for the original stone lintel. Murphy's conversion turned a modest, unremarkable and rather run-down structure into a compact but surprisingly spacious town house where new materials are used decisively but in harmony with the old fabric. The spatial ingenuity of the scheme is strongly reminiscent of Murphy's beloved Scarpa.

Murphy's instinct was 'to accept the building as we found it, but then to express the new use within it, so that it became a building within a building'. The basic format of the mews elevation remained unchanged: the handsome stonework was simply cleaned and repointed. Using the first floor as living space, however, posed problems: the head height in the old hayloft was inadequate. The demolition of the existing floor structure allowed a new floor level to be established, expressed externally by means of a steel beam within the existing opening. The beam provided a runner for the new garage door – planners demanded that parking for one car be provided within the house. Glass blocks are used to fill the entrance hall with daylight.

The new house is conceived as a continuous space that makes maximum use of available daylight – precious in this northern location – which is supplied from a rooflight, supplemented by mirrors (which add to the spatial effects). The kitchen and dining space are on the ground floor, with the main living area and bedroom above, but there are vertical and horizontal views through all the spaces. Built-in furniture, designed by the architects, includes sliding elements that can be used to screen off parts of the interior. Timber is used extensively, in conjunction with simply detailed steel sections for handrails and other fixtures.

The scheme succeeds on two levels. Firstly, it preserves the modest identity of the original as an unassuming element in a workaday mews. Secondly, it offers a remarkably enjoyable experience in city living within the framework of the old building and capitalizes with great skill on resources of space and light. This is architecture in miniature of a high order.

Cross-section

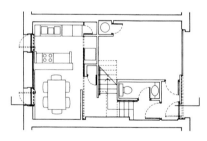

Ground-floor plan

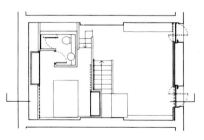

First-floor plan

BRITISH COUNCIL OFFICES AND THE ERICSSON PALACE CONVERSION PRAGUE, CZECH REPUBLIC

JESTICO & WHILES, 1991–97

The British practice Jestico & Whiles began operations in Prague soon after the collapse of Communism. The following two schemes reflect the city's openness in the aftermath of the 'Velvet Revolution'. The building in which the British Council established its new cultural centre and offices was a significant example of 1920s Czech functionalism, but had been badly altered during the years it was owned by the former East German authorities. The Council's operations are located on the ground and lower ground floor of the building and include a reading room, library and small cinema as well as administrative offices. The restored ground-floor atrium, accessed by a passageway from the street that once housed small shops, is the centre of the Council's activities, and is freely open to the general public. The glazed roof was carefully reinstated. Its centrepiece is a big glass reading table – actually a rooflight into the library below. The glass-block floor to the atrium had survived, though covered over, and was repaired and reinstated. The offices are defined by steel screens, glazed in white and blue glass, again promoting a feel of openness and accessibility. The scheme was far from extravagant – propriety was more important than display – but was intended to show a regard for the local tradition of modern design.

The Ericsson Palace block was an accretion of work dating from the twelfth century onwards and included some impressive Gothic and Baroque interiors, though all had been much altered behind later façades. Jestico & Whiles' transformation focused on the central courtyard, a forgotten space now rediscovered. The use of a retractable roof made this space usable regardless of the weather. Much of the basic structure of the block was in poor condition – many of the upper floors faced collapse – but sound beams were salvaged and recycled in the conversion, which provided residential, office and retail space. The aim underlying the new work was to achieve great lightness and transparency and to avoid any pastiche of the old.

MEDIA CENTRE HAMBURG, GERMANY

ME DI UM ARCHITEKTEN, 1983–92

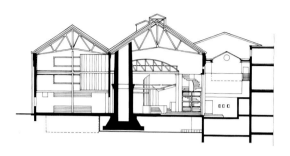

facing page: View through the building, showing the underside of its glass 'prow'.
above: Cross-section.

Despite heavy wartime bombing, the great port of Hamburg retains many monuments of nineteenth-century commerce and industry. Until 1979 – when it went into receivership – the Zeise factory in the industrial suburb of Ottensen was a living relic of Hamburg's maritime history. The factory was founded in 1868 by Theodor Zeise and produced propellers for ships. The Zeise empire expanded under Theodor Zeise's son Alfred and flourished into the post-Second World War period. With the closure of its operations, the sprawling factory complex (or *Zeisehallen*) was abandoned, with historic machinery salvaged for a local industrial museum. If preservation of the factory itself, largely late nineteenth- and early twentieth-century in date, was ever an option, it quickly receded as the buildings became subject to vandalism and natural decay. Within a few years, they were utterly derelict. In any case, the policy of the city – which scheduled the remains as a protected monument – was to see the factory reused, rather than embalmed.

The planning and architectural practice of me di um (under partners Thiess Jentz, Heiko Popp and Peter Wiesner) combines the design of innovative new buildings with a radical approach to reuse which bears comparison with, for example, that of Los Angeles architect Eric Owen Moss at Culver City. For me di um, the existing fabric demanded retention and respect, but formed a context for new work which is non-deferential – indeed, forceful – in its impact on the old.

Me di um became involved with the site in the early 1980s, when city planners took a bold initiative to retrieve it from irreparable ruin. The architects worked with developers Procomon on a phased refurbishment scheme aimed at the burgeoning local film and multimedia scene and encouraged by the public-funded Hamburger Filmbüro.

Stripped of their rusting machinery and a mass of debris (including partly collapsed roofs), the buildings in the *Zeisehallen* emerged as grand and simple spaces, with a raw dignity that demanded a decisive response from the reuse process. The buildings were ranged around a central factory yard off the Friedensallee and their distinctive forms encouraged a gradualist approach based on a mix of uses. The Eisenstein restaurant was the pioneering venture on the site, located in a building on the factory yard converted, in 1986–88, by me di um (winners of a 1986 competition) working in association with Peter Dinse and Isabell Feest. The aesthetic of the restaurant interior is uncompromisingly industrial – the base of a large furnace chimney is a dominating presence. The most significant intervention, the bar, is a strong element in its own right, its thrusting 'prow' a clear reference to the nautical associations of the site. The substantial block behind the restaurant was subsequently converted to house the Film and Theatre Institute, complete with a library open to the public. Shops, offices, studios, 60 flats and a three-screen cinema block were developed elsewhere on the site. The cinema intrudes its great curved façade into the rectangular grid of the old factory, its solid form contrasting with the spare elegance of the stripped-back brick, steel and glass industrial setting. New structures within are generally free-form and explicitly sculptural, 'soft architecture' overlying a sturdy skeleton of old work. Within the Film Institute, new offices sit in cabin-like boxes within the structural grid.

A conscious – it might even be said, self-conscious – effort was made to retain the ethos of industry in the revamped buildings, with pockmarked brickwork, left as found, and sawn-off steel beams freely displayed. The aim is not simply to retain a memory of the industrial past but to stress the clear break between old and new work. The architects speak of the project in terms of 'a city within the city' – new 'streets' and 'squares' have been constructed within the envelope of the old complex. The retention of substantial areas of public and semi-public space, usually full height and day-lit from the refurbished glazed roofs, enhances the impression of genuine urban space. With the relocation of Hamburg University's prestigious faculty of film and theatre to the *Zeisehallen*, the sense of community has been intensified – the buildings are in use around the clock. The project provides for a dynamic sense of movement around the site. There is no sense of a cultural ghetto: the public is encouraged to enter the block, which is penetrated by a new public arcade, lined with shops cut through the old buildings (though the recycled *Zeisehallen* has been compared to a self-sufficient walled city).

The Media Centre is now an established part of the life of the city – as a working factory, it had been a private, closed domain. It exemplifies the role of 'cultural industries' in urban regeneration in the aftermath of more traditional industries. Me di um's achievement has been to create a highly flexible framework for living, working and relaxing in a building that, far from being smoothed over or sanitized, continues to express the dignity of manufacture.

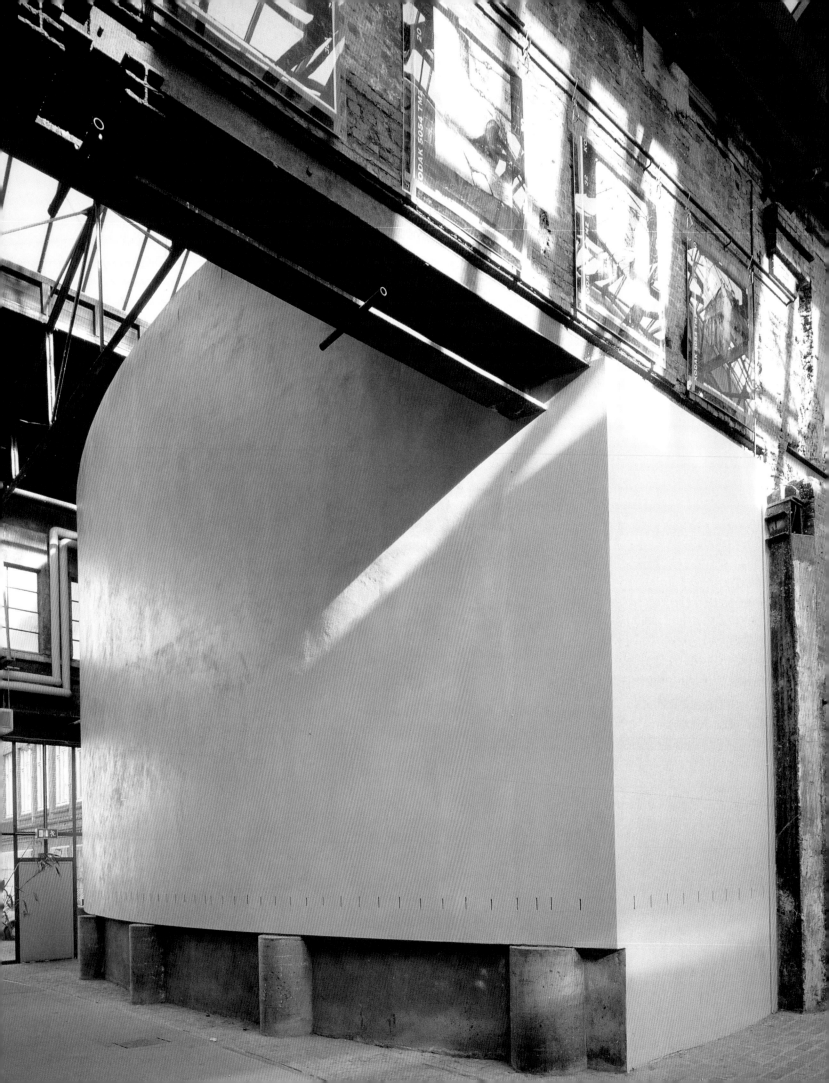

facing page: New elements are freestanding structures within the building: view of the cinema's curved façade.

above: The Zeise propeller factory in Hamburg had become almost terminally derelict before its conversion into a media centre.

HOPE Center for Advanced Technologies DETROIT, USA

SHG INCORPORATED, 1994

facing page: The HOPE Center makes use of a spacious 1930s factory – the internal space has been little changed, except for the insertion of a series of towers which contain services as well as teaching spaces.

Detroit is a classic 'rustbelt' city, hit by the decline and reconfiguration of traditional manufacturing industries. It has a large number of redundant industrial buildings, mostly dating from the early twentieth century. The HOPE Center makes use of a high quality 1930s factory (attributed to Albert Kahn) as the base for an innovative training facility, part of a government-backed campaign to regenerate the local economy and tackle high levels of youth unemployment. Young people, drawn from inner-city schools, are trained in computer-integrated manufacturing skills. The centre manufactures as well as educates, however, supplying parts to the car industry and effectively paying for its own running costs.

The existing building was a classic configuration of its era, very widely reproduced throughout North America and Europe: a 16,700 square-metre (180,000 square-foot) single-storey manufacturing block fronted by a three-storey, 3,700 square-metre (40,000 square-foot) office and administration wing, forming a show frontage to the street. Project architect William Hartman admired the quality of the building, but saw it as 'an enclosure, a functional space for machines to operate, supplemented by humans'. The focus of the new training facility, in contrast, was to be people.

The intention was to challenge the traditional factory ethos within the existing structure and with a relatively modest ($22 million) construction budget. The great expanse of the production floor was divided into six distinct neighbourhoods, each containing 15 workspace cells. These are serviced by three-storey 'power towers', containing an air-handling plant and lavatories, plus computer classrooms. The towers help to promote a sense of location and identity within a very large building. The only major change to the existing envelope was the raising of the roof of the factory floor (where it meets the office wing) to create a light-filled three-storey atrium with a viewing platform that provides an overview of the whole workspace. (Half a century ago, there was a rigid divide between offices and the factory floor which is now irrelevant.) The office wing itself has been converted into teaching and conference space, with an 'electronic library' on the second floor.

The architects' approach to transformation was to respect the existing fabric, but to add a layer of colour and graphic identity – the bold Corbusier-inspired numerals on the power towers, for example – as well as up-to-date services. The high-energy profile of the old factory was unacceptable – the reuse project recycles waste heat from a natural gas-powered system and saves heavily on running costs. The roof has been provided with greatly augmented insulation to reduce energy loss. Lighting is now task-related, rather than universal – high-intensity fixtures come into operation only when the machines they serve are in use. The uniform overlighting of the old-style factory floor has been banished.

SHG Incorporated's scheme, though free of gimmicks and pragmatic in its aims, has transformed a symbol of industrial decline into an emblem of regeneration. In functional terms, the building has been re-equipped for its new role. But the quietly stylish approach to refurbishment has made the old factory a morale-booster in its own right.

The only significant change to the existing structure was the insertion of a three-storey atrium,
the 'super-tooth', under a raised roof where the former production and office spaces meet.

Elevation

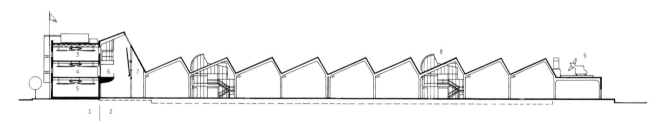

Cross-section

1	Existing three-storey office building	6	Visitor's centre platform
2	Existing manufacturing building	7	Supertooth bracing and display screen
3	Meeting room	8	Power tower
4	Conference room	9	Communications link
5	Locker room		

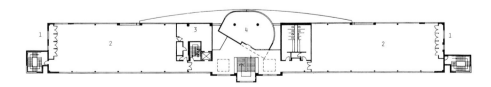

Third-floor plan

1	Storage	3	Service pantry
2	Meeting room	4	Special meeting room

Nestlé Headquarters NOISIEL, MARNE-LA-VALLÉE, FRANCE

REICHEN & ROBERT ARCHITECTES, 1993–96

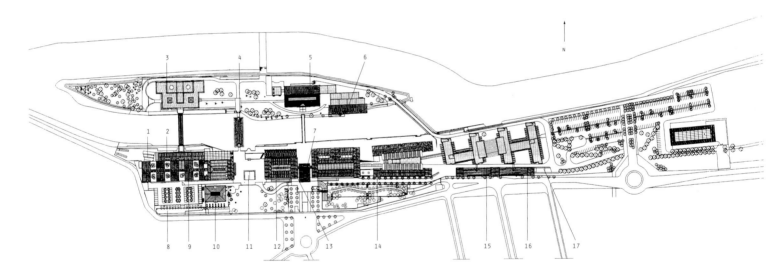

Site plan

1	Warehouse	10	*Halle Eiffel*
2	Customer services	11	Conference rooms
3	*Cathédrale*	12	Shop
4	The mill	13	Security
5	Restaurants	14	Travel agency
6	Cafeteria	15	Medical centre
7	Reception	16	Maintenance
8	Photographic studio	17	Warehouse
9	Garage		

left: Poyet's watercolour of the Menier chocolate factory in the late 1860s.
right: The mill is a striking focus point for the Nestlé France headquarters.

For a decade or more, Reichen & Robert have set the pace in the sphere of architectural transformation in France. Their particular expertise lies in the reuse of industrial buildings, where their unswerving respect for nineteenth-century engineering achievements and incisive approach to innovative new design, eschewing pastiche, has underpinned the regeneration process. By any standard, however, the Nestlé Headquarters is a big project, embracing 60,000 square metres (645,834 square feet) of buildings and costing around FF800 million. It is incontestably one of the most significant transformational projects of the 1990s and all the more remarkable because the context was one of France's key industrial monuments. The factory at Noisiel, on the river Marne, was founded in the 1820s by Jean Menier, initially as a pharmaceutical works and subsequently to make chocolate. The complex of buildings grew steadily over the next century. The additions of the 1860s by Jules Saulnier (wrought-iron framed buildings clad in stone and patterned brick) culminated in the new mill of 1872–74, clad in elaborate brickwork and sitting on beams spanning the Marne. The top floor of the mill featured a suspended floor structure, free of columns. Further extensions took place in the 1880s, when Gustave Eiffel engineered the new engine house (the *Halle Eiffel*). The so-called *Cathédrale* of 1906–8 (engineered by Armand Considère) was built on the Hennebique reinforced concrete system, with a daringly slim concrete bridge linking it to the main factory across the river. The factory was the centrepiece of the Menier domain, which included the family residence, workers' housing, farmland, woods and recreational parks. In the best paternalistic tradition, the Meniers aimed to give their workers a healthy and attractive working environment and the quality of the buildings was a source of pride – they were seen consciously as a symbol and a showpiece.

The eventual absorption of the company into the Nestlé empire (no longer confined to chocolate) led to the rundown and (in 1993) the closure of the Noisiel factory. Demolition of the buildings was ruled out. There were ideas of developing the site as a business park – Reichen & Robert were commissioned in 1993 to draw up plans for conversion – but Nestlé's own management shake-up led to the decision that the company would itself occupy the buildings as headquarters for its French operations. The strong image of the place and the attraction of its riverside setting (a short drive from the centre of Paris) impressed the Nestlé executives, while the variety of the buildings offered identities for the various Nestlé divisions to be located at Noisiel. Construction work began in February 1994 and 1,750 staff moved in two years later.

Noisiel was conceived as a 'campus', with a number of shared facilities such as restaurants, and even an urban quarter with a network of streets and squares around the buildings. Strict restoration was one part of the programme – the *Monuments Historiques* took direct charge of the mill exterior, with the interior mostly containing a boardroom and directors' suites. The main driving force, however, was not preservation but change. Around 19,000 square metres (204,514 square feet) of new buildings were constructed on the eastern edge of the site. The old buildings were reconfigured to meet the needs of an entirely new set of users. Additions and insertions to the old buildings made no attempt at 'keeping in keeping', but were in a timeless tradition of unselfconscious industrial design – and therefore immediately seemed at home in their surroundings. The architects aimed at a dialogue between old and new and had no qualms about using materials, such as stainless steel and sanded glass, unknown in the nineteenth century. Nor was there any hesitation about using colour in the recast interiors. The aim was to create rich and enjoyable spaces, far removed from conventional office anonymity.

When the building existed as a chocolate factory, the raw materials and finished products were moved in and out of the site on a system of internal railways snaking through the buildings. The railway routes have now become covered pedestrian arcades for circulation around the site. In places, the changes have been radical. Some buildings, mainly recent in date, were demolished. Others have been internally so recast that they appear new, such as an auditorium, formed out of concrete cooling vaults. The Eiffel engine house and the *Cathédrale* have, however, been retained in a restored but unaltered state as exhibition and reception space. The general ambience is one of contrast, between old fabric and new fitout and furnishing – in general, the aim was to make the changes reversible. Reichen & Robert's stylish pragmatism, rooted in the engineering tradition, proved to be perfectly suited to Noisiel, and is their most significant work to date.

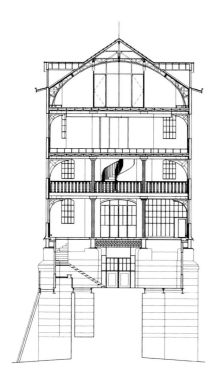

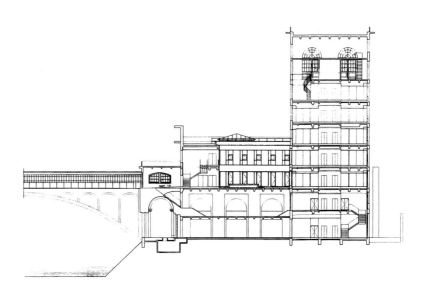

facing page: Floors within the Saulnier mill are linked by remarkably elegant iron staircases.

above: Section through Saulnier's famous iron-framed mill of 1872–74, which spans the river Marne.

right: Section through the *Cathédrale*, built in 1906–8 on a reinforced concrete frame.

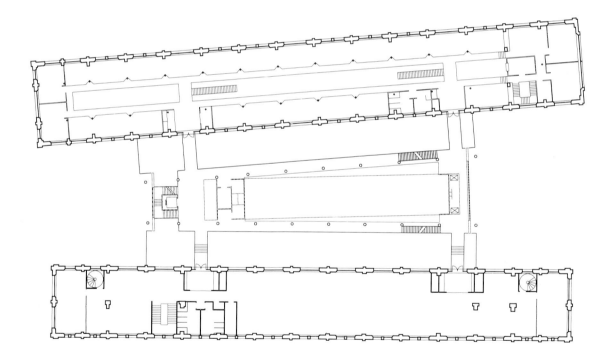

above: The 'naves' of the former factory blocks have been converted into two- and three-storey office spaces and linked by new glazed atria.

facing page: The new internal spaces of the 'naves' are daylit, with bridges linking upper floors.

In both the *Cathédrale* (left) and the *Halle Eiffel* (right), internal spaces have been
carefully preserved and restored to provide exhibition and reception areas.

The various blocks are linked by a series of lightweight glazed structures, designed in
an entirely contemporary manner.

CULVER CITY LOS ANGELES, USA

ERIC OWEN MOSS ARCHITECTS, 1979–

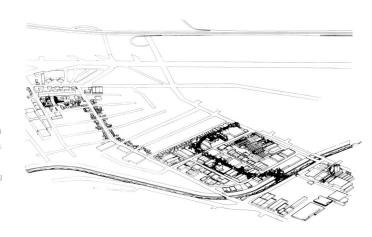

right: Aerial view of the Culver City area, where Eric Owen Moss has transformed a series of redundant industrial and commercial blocks to provide offices and studios in radically adapted spaces.

facing page: The Samitaur block at Culver City, a new block built across an existing building, is entered via a dramatic cone, or cylinder, which contains a staircase extending to roof level.

Eric Owen Moss is a symbolic and formative figure in late twentieth-century Los Angeles architecture, whose reputation has been almost entirely forged in the conversion of existing buildings, notably in the Culver City area, close to south-central Los Angeles, which was once a centre of film making. The availability of cheap, redundant studio and warehouse buildings opened the way for a radical transformation of the city fabric, though the potential was only realized when an imaginative, risk-taking developer – Frederick Smith – appeared. Over the last two decades, Moss and Smith have been instrumental in the regeneration of this quarter of the city. The raw material was 'good, ordinary' buildings, with resource value but of no special historic or architectural interest.

Moss's campaign of transformation at Culver City began in an ad hoc spirit – a reflection of the realities of the site. His philosophy of architecture is rooted in a philosophy of the city. But a coherent plan for the area has steadily emerged. The Ince complex, close to the Santa Monica Freeway, provided the focus for Moss's earlier work in Culver City and included the conversion of the former Paramount Laundry into offices for a design firm; the remodelling of a derelict warehouse into the Lindblade Tower workspaces (with a striking new tower to give identity to a utilitarian structure); and the Gary Group Building, providing offices for an advertising agency. A feature of the latter is the insertion into the roof structure of two large metal and glass funnels, feeding natural light into the building. The fourth element in the complex was the offices for the Metafor media company, formed in a 836 square-metre (9,000 square-foot) concrete warehouse, built on a trapezoidal plan. The key 'event' of the conversion is the new staircase inserted at the south-west corner of the block, providing access to upper floors. The Ince project has culminated in the proposed Ince Theatre, which Moss envisages as 'a hypodermic to the new downtown'.

Moss's gradual reconfiguration of the Hayden Tract area of Culver City continues at 8522 National Boulevard, where five warehouses dating from the 1920s to the 1940s were transformed by Frederick Smith into offices and design studios. Key issues in the conversion were the provision of daylight and of access into the deep-plan structures. New 'causeways', streets and piazzas open up the

interiors. Natural light enters largely from above, providing luminous and often dramatic spaces which are 'carved' out of the existing mass. The elliptical meeting room in one of the blocks, where curved plywood walls and a new plaster ceiling are superimposed on the bare concrete of the original structure, has become a familiar image of the scheme and of contemporary American architecture. Throughout the scheme, new work and old are interlaced and interlayered – sometimes 'colliding' in a way that is far from accidental. Moss has praised the work of his developer client, who was 'ready to let his conception – or the architect's conception – direct the selling, as opposed to letting the selling direct the architecture'.

The Pittard Sullivan (PS) building at Hayden Tract continues the themes of the earlier conversion projects. Foremost is the idea that modern office space can colonize space that was built for a very different purpose. The steel-framed industrial building is stripped back to its metallic bones and a new steel structure inserted to support new floors. Partitions, screens and bridges divide up and interconnect the new spaces. There is an emphasis, as usual in Moss's work, on colour, expressive form and the texture of materials (though Moss himself has recanted on the 'hedonism' of some of the earlier work). The existing buildings are treated as raw material, not untouchable monuments. More recent projects, notably SPARCITY, reject the tyranny of street and block. In this instance, a redundant rail track is the base for an 'air rights' development which is at odds with the established topography.

Eric Owen Moss's work at Culver City and elsewhere in Los Angeles has little to do with conventional ideas of adaptive reuse. As Moss declared of 8522 National Boulevard, 'the original building has some presence in the solution. But the degree of that presence is up to you. You can't eradicate all of it, so you have to try to understand it. It's like starting to work on a page that is not blank'. These words sum up the enormous potential of architectural transformation, of which Moss is a consummate master: to make 'nowhere' into 'somewhere'. 'Sometimes the job is to defend the new from the old', he has written. 'Sometimes to put the old together with the new.'

left: Inside, the Samitaur block is notable for its strongly modelled entrance 'cone'.
right: The Samitaur building belongs to a later phase of the project and combines refurbishment with new building in a seamless, if hardly relaxed, whole.

left: Moss's interiors are never straightforward – in the Samitaur block, they are almost
Baroque in their complexity.

right: Moss's project at Culver City began with the Ince Complex, where the Gary Group
building is a prominent landmark.

above: The exterior of the Gary Group building epitomizes Moss's approach – celebrating the ordinariness of what exists, yet subtly subverting it with bold new interventions.

facing page: At the Pittard Sullivan building, new elements are exaggerated and deliberately, even wilfully designed for maximum impact. The intention is architectural, but the effects are fortuitous in the context of an area whose rundown image needed to be jettisoned.

following page: The Pittard Sullivan building has been stripped back to its frame and recast with entirely new spaces hung over a new steel structure and interconnected by bridges. The size of the building has increased, but it has equally become something more than a purely functional container.

CHAPTER 2
LEISURE & LEARNING

The recolonization of the city, a process set to continue into the twenty-first century, is about rediscovery. Buildings that once seemed doomed to permanent disuse and eventual destruction are now perceived as having financial and social value. The change of attitudes to old buildings reflects a change in attitudes to the city and to urban life. Jane Jacobs, whose pioneering defence of the value of old buildings is now regarded as a classic statement of the new urbanism, listed the diverse activities carried on in the New York block where she lived. 'There is no place for the likes of us in new construction', Jacobs wrote, 'and the last thing we need is new construction.'[1] The rationale of Jacobs's argument was eventually conceded, not only in New York but in many other cities. (In Birmingham, England, for example, the proposed clearance of the Jewellery Quarter was abandoned after it was realized that it would probably cause fatal damage to the city's jewellery industry, which depended on a supply of cheap space, close to the central area.) The significance of old buildings and areas for the survival of small businesses that cannot afford to relocate – and which function well in close proximity to each other – has now been realized. Yet old industries contract and die. Areas of Manhattan that were purely industrial 30 years ago have been colonized by art galleries, cafés and bars and by new residents unable to afford the ultimate chic of a SoHo or TriBeCa loft. So-called 'cultural industries' have brought new life to many city areas left high and dry by economic change. The Marais district of Paris is a special instance, reprieved and restored by a state initiative, but the costly official projects – including Yves Lion's European House of Photography (pages 168–173) – have been greatly outnumbered by the small-scale, privately-funded restoration and reuse schemes which have brought a decaying area back to life. Every big city has areas where culture – or, often, the youth-oriented anti-culture represented by the world of clubs and bars – has proved the key to revival. 'Fringe' theatre thrives in old buildings. The Roundhouse, a former engine shed in north London, a legendary venue for rock concerts, experimental theatre and art installations over the last 40 years, is now set to become an arts centre for children. The great Halle des Boeufs at Paris's Parc de la Villette is another spectacular music venue – La Villette, once a huge abattoir, is now one of the mainstays of the Paris arts scene. Bernard Tschumi's extraordinary National Studio for Contemporary Arts at Le Fresnoy (pages 134–141) points the way to a future in which old and new structures are interlocked to create a fertile new urban form. In effect, Tschumi's project is entirely conservationist, yet its motivation comes from elsewhere – from a conviction about living in cities and enjoying the layers of complexity and richness that they contain. The old is transformed to serve new generations, not destroyed. Destruction is a negative, conservative move – transformation is the way for the future.

1. J. Jacobs, *Death and Life of Great American Cities*, New York 1961, p. 206

P.S.1 INSTITUTE FOR CONTEMPORARY ART LONG ISLAND CITY, NEW YORK, USA

FREDERICK FISHER & PARTNERS ARCHITECTS, 1994–97

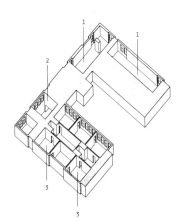

First-floor art spaces.

1   Galleries
2   Duplex gallery
3   'Classroom' galleries

facing page: The 1890s school building stands in an area close to central Manhattan but is itself in need of regeneration and renewal.
following page: The conversion has retained much of the character of the building.

P.S.1 – the initials stand for 'public school' – is not a new institution. It was founded in the mid-1970s by Alanna Heiss, a New York-based collector and curator who has long campaigned, through the Institute for Contemporary Art, for the use of abandoned city-owned buildings as venues for art and workplaces for artists. (Her first exhibition utilized the spaces below the Brooklyn Bridge.) The former public school in Long Island City, just across the Queensboro Bridge from Manhattan, a 9,300 square-metre (100,000 square-foot) monument in robust neo-Romanesque style, had been abandoned when Heiss discovered it and persuaded the City of New York to transfer it to the Institute.

The major renovation by California-based Frederick Fisher has, however, finally realized the full potential of the building, itself a not inconsiderable work of art. Respect for the building and a concern to express its history were key strengths of the Fisher project, demonstrating once more the particular appropriateness of old buildings for the display of avant-garde art. The $8 million renovation budget was modest by New York standards, but the aims behind P.S.1 have always been rather different from some of Manhattan's more eminent galleries. (Providing studio space for working artists for example has always been part of its role.)

The original school building was constructed in two phases; the first was completed in 1890 and employed a traditional load-bearing construction; the second was completed in 1900 on a steel frame, which allowed for wider spans. Fisher's aim was to strip down the building to its original form, removing later accretions, revealing history and maximizing usable space. Original finishes, such as linoleum tiles in corridors and original paint colours, were restored wherever possible. Old wood-block floors were retained and repaired. Public areas were left as 'school'. In contrast, the galleries have been kept a pristine white, as they were in the 1970s. Varied in size and shape, one gallery occupies the former boiler room while others are located in corridors. In the wing dating from 1900, one gallery extends across an entire floor.

The conventional idea of an art gallery is turned upside down. Opening up the building physically was seen to be as important as opening it up metaphorically: to provide a fresh audience with forward-looking ideas. The new outdoor galleries extend the exhibition spaces into the open air while the main entrance has been completely redesigned to express openness. The renovation of P.S.1 reveals a determination rare among architects to let the use, rather than the building, predominate. According to Alanna Heiss, 'we made a real effort to keep in mind that we are housed in a school, that we are an art centre and that we want to be a home for art, rather than a prized tourist attraction'. The building should not, she argued, be the centre of attention. In the age of the Getty in California and the Guggenheim in Bilbao, such a view sounds revolutionary.

left: The tough spaces of the old school provide an adaptable setting for experimental art works. No attempt has been made to erase the ethos of an inner-city school.

right: Duplex gallery. A floor level was taken out to create a double-height space for showing large three-dimensional art works, allowing views down from the first floor. The original wall surface has been stripped away to reveal the underlying nature of the building.

The second phase of the school, completed in 1900, used reinforced concrete
construction and has large-span spaces ideal for display purposes.

PUBLIC LIBRARY SALAMANCA, SPAIN

VÍCTOR LÓPEZ COTELO ARQUITECTO WITH CARLOS PUENTE FERNÁNDEZ, 1984–93

The imposing palace known as the Casa de las Conchas ('House of Shells'), in the heart of Salamanca, was earmarked for conversion to a new public library in 1984. The project took a decade, but is distinguished for its exceptional balance of strict restoration and innovative new work. Meticulously detailed, the library is an exemplary expression of the Spanish concern to knit history and regeneration together.

The Casa de las Conchas is a venerable landmark of the university city of Salamanca. Built in the late fifteenth century by Don Rodrigo Maldonado de Talavera, scholar and royal counsellor (who piously decorated its façade with the scallop shells associated with the shrine of St James at Compostela), it was altered and enriched by his son and further recast in the eighteenth century, when one of the façades (facing on to the calle de la Rua) was extensively rebuilt with regular square windows, in place of the more picturesque Gothic openings. In more recent years, under municipal ownership, the palace fell into disuse and near-dereliction. With the public excluded on safety grounds, the central government was obliged to consider possible new uses. It was decided to locate a public library within the building, a bold move given the special interest of the fabric and the likely imposition of constraints on the process of reuse.

The first priority was to halt the process of deterioration. Roofs were in a poor state, with timbers threatened by rot. Stonework was badly weathered. More seriously, there were subsidence problems caused by defective foundations. This produced cracking of the masonry and brought parts of the building – notably its superb central courtyard – close to collapse. At this stage, the task was essentially restorative. The repair process was slow and painstaking and included reinforcement of the foundations, major stone repairs and partial replacement of masonry, along with cleaning and repointing, repair of the roof structures (including the removal of later insertions done in steel), a complete overhaul of roof coverings and the partial dismantling and reassembly of the collapsing arcades of the courtyard. These measures were needed merely to preserve a historic monument, but preservation was not the sole motive. Within the repaired structure, the architects integrated a scheme of reuse that gave the building an assured future.

The brief was for a sizeable lending library, with a smaller reference and research division. To provide all the facilities needed, the space available had to be used to the full – indeed, it became necessary to extend the building. The public entrance is on the calle de la Compania. Readers cross the restored courtyard (also freely accessible to sightseers) to a security point, controlling access to the library. Most readers use the general reading room, a new timber, steel and glass structure – really a refined shed – freestanding in what was originally an open courtyard. Another new intervention provides a link at ground-floor level to the lending stacks. Five floors of open access stacks are contained within the wing on the calle de la Rua and accessed by a new staircase, or lifts. Cross-walls were removed in this wing to provide a unified space. The research library is on the first and second floors, with administration on the third floor. An auditorium and small exhibition area have been provided at basement level, where there are also staff facilities. Handsome brick vaults have been cleaned and repaired. Access to the library is internal, not via the external court – allowing unmonitored access to the latter for the public and tourists, who do not interfere with the operations of the library.

Cotelo & Puente's approach to the fitout of the building is refined without being minimal. There is a strong emphasis on the use of timber for new elements. In a new second-floor periodicals room, a finely crafted timber ceiling evokes, without copying, the character of surviving medieval ceilings in the building. Timber floors have been widely used. New furnishings are simple and elegant. The approach to the installation of services has been towards discretion and integration, rather than display. Externally, the use of handsome wooden shutters provides protection from the hot summer sun and something of the sense of privacy and exclusion traditional in the great private palaces of Spain. The Casa de las Conchas has gained a new role, without losing its aura, as one of the hidden treasures of Salamanca.

left: The Casa de las Conchas is one of the most important historic buildings in Salamanca –
its name derives from the use of shells as a decorative feature on the fifteenth-century façade.
right: The courtyard was inaccessible for some years, after the building fell into disuse.

left: The detailing is refined, with a strong emphasis on timber for new elements.
right: Basement stack, showing cleaned and refurbished brick vaulting together with a new lighting scheme.

The general reading room is a freestanding timber, steel and glass
structure occupying an internal court.

Cotelo and Puente's new interventions are invisible from surrounding streets and from
the courtyard, but provide essential links to facilitate reuse as a public library.

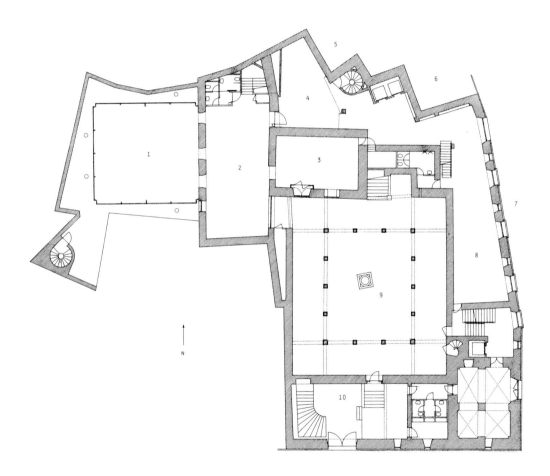

Ground-floor plan

1	Reading room	6	Exhibition space
2	Card catalogue	7	Staff entrance
3	Entrance check point	8	Public stacks
4	Exit check point	9	Public entrance
5	Auditorium	10	Cloister

THE CITADEL LOS ANGELES, USA

THE NADEL PARTNERSHIP AND SUSSMAN/PREJZA & COMPANY, INC. WITH MARTHA SCHWARTZ, 1990-91

Los Angeles is renowned for the extraordinary range of its architectural heritage, which has sometimes veered towards the explicitly fantastic and even bizarre. This heritage has too often been undervalued and some famous landmarks have been randomly destroyed – even today, preservation is not a typically Angeleno pursuit.

The Samson (later Uniroyal) Tire and Rubber Company's plant on the Santa Ana Freeway, 9 kilometres (6 miles) east of downtown LA, was extreme even by the standards of its own day. Its 518 metre- (1,700 foot-) long frontage, constructed of concrete and completed in 1929 to designs by Morgan, Walls & Clements – in 'Mesopotamian' (or 'Assyro-Babylonian') style – was clearly inspired by cinema epics and was actually used as a backdrop for scenes in *Ben Hur*. Well loved though the building was, it rapidly fell into abject decay after the factory closed in 1978.

Rescue came via a mixed-use scheme – offices, hotel and discount retail operation – for the 14 hectare (35 acre) site, devised by the Nadel Partnership. The retail element became the key component in the transformation of the derelict site and has worked very well, perhaps because exceptional designers were brought in to mould it. The architectural ingredient in the original buildings was, in fact, quite small: behind the elaborate frontage (a marketing device, pure and simple) lay areas of utilitarian sheds. The frontage (which other potential developers proposed to demolish) was carefully restored, together with an area of offices located at its centre. The new 14,585 square-metre (157,000 square-foot) retail mall is located to one side of a new avenue providing access through the site – the offices are on the other side – created by demolishing a section of the 1929 façade. This was a bold move, but it was seen as vital in opening up the site to a motorized public which had always seen the frontage as an impermeable barrier. In the new design, the façade is expressed as a prop, as flimsy as a movie set but no less remarkable for that.

Landscape designer Martha Schwartz was commissioned to lay out the new avenue, using evenly planted palm trees set in concrete bases formed on the model of old tyres, with grey and red paving used to denote pedestrian and vehicular space. The design pays homage to the gardens of Babylon as well as to West Coast mythology. Mixing cars and people was seen as risky, but it works: although there is a vast parking area (planted with olive trees) to the rear of the site, drivers are now allowed through the 'front door'.

Sussman/Prejza's work on the retail mall included the revamping of retained elements of the old factory, such as the food court, as well as large areas of new construction. The approach is frankly eclectic, mixing industrial and vernacular elements that are unified with the use of bold colour in the best Californian tradition. The use of coloured stucco reflects the indigenous buildings of the region, as does the proliferation of small, shaded external courts. A landmark tower is modelled on the form of the oil derricks found in the area. What the project as a whole lacks in conventional good taste (not an issue on the LA freeways) is made up for by its recreation of the spirit of invention and fantasy that motivated the site's original developers. What could have been a mundane commercial development has been given a flavour of the extraordinary. The merging together of old and new has resulted in a fresh LA landmark.

113

above: The 'Mesopotamian' style façade has been preserved and restored as part of the transformation scheme. The 'ziggurat' now houses offices.

facing page: Behind the street front, most of the factory sheds have been cleared and a new landscaped avenue, designed by Martha Schwartz, provides access to the development.

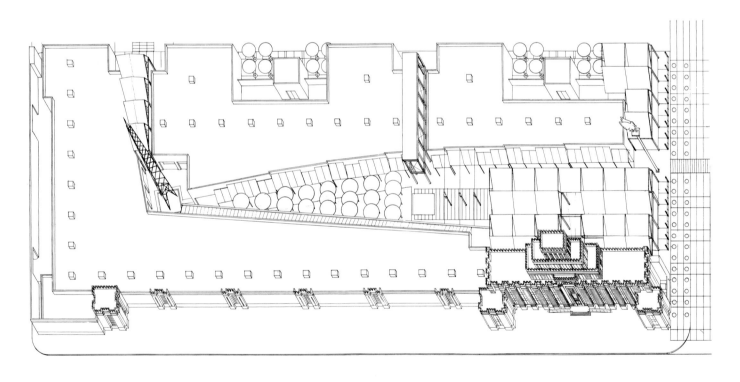

View of the historic Samson building and the food court.

A substantial area of the old factory has been retained for the new retail development,
just as new structures are contained within the old fabric.

CENTRE FOR ART AND MEDIA TECHNOLOGY KARLSRUHE, GERMANY

ARCHITEKTEN SCHWEGER & PARTNER, 1993–99

facing page: The façade of the former munitions factory is juxtaposed with the modernity of Schweger & Partner's addition. A conduit containing services links the two buildings.

The background to Schweger & Partner's spectacular conversion of a vast armaments factory into a home for the innovative Centre for Art and Media Technology was the collapse of a high-profile new-build scheme. A 1989 competition to design a building to house the centre had been won by Rem Koolhaas and the project attracted international interest. There was local concern, however, about the likely fate of the munitions factory, close to the centre of Karlsruhe, which was built in 1915–18 to designs by P. J. Manz.

Nearly 304 metres (1,000 feet) long, the building was a major landmark. Its handsome, vernacular-style façades concealed some grim memories, however: the factory had been abandoned after the First World War, but had played a major role in the German war effort under Hitler, when thousands of slave labourers from Eastern Europe were forced to work there. Having survived wartime bombing, the factory was colonized by a number of users but in the 1980s plans were announced for its clearance. The faceless character of much new development around the factory fuelled demands for its retention. After much thought, the city resolved to locate the Centre for Art and Media Technology there, and to cancel the Koolhaas scheme.

The original Manz building was rigidly planned as a series of toplit full-height production spaces, laid out as ten inner courts surrounded by multi-level blocks. These big, simple spaces with ample natural light had clear potential for reuse.

The continuing conversion project provides premises for an art and design college, modern art museum, media museum and (yet to be completed) for the City Art Gallery, with its historic collection. The toplit courtyards provide space for circulation and for visitor amenities, including cafés, with galleries in the surrounding wings. The general approach has been to let the old fabric speak for itself, with few interventions; the industrial ambience is in keeping with much of the work displayed. The lightness of the steel staircases and galleries results in a high degree of transparency.

The determination to live with the past is marked – in places, the railway tracks that ran right into the production spaces can still be seen. Schweger & Partner's scheme was designed to make optimum use of a large and solid building without impinging on its existing character. As such, it is only marginally transformational in intent. Yet there was a clear need to express the fact that the building had a new use, and that its unhappy past could be laid aside. The 'blue cube' that has become the emblem of the new institution performs precisely this role. It contains a highly adaptable performance space and features a double skin – glazing on the exterior with metal panels, painted blue, within. There have been suggestions that the 'cube' is a reference to the lost Koolhaas building, a compensation for the cancellation of a modern masterwork. It is certainly a marker of change.

Eröffnung
18. Oktober 1997

Schweger & Partner's 'blue cube' contains a flexible performance space, and has become a symbol of the new Centre for Art and Media Technology.

The full-height courts were surrounded by multi-storey wings –
the mix of spaces was ideal for the new use.

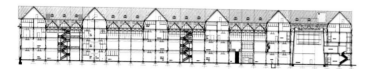

P. J. Manz's factory, built in 1915–18, was arranged around a series of internal courts.

1   Exhibition spaces
2   Shop
3   Foyer
4   Media theatre
5   Studio

6   Offices
7   Film and video studios
8   Entrance
9   'Blue cube'

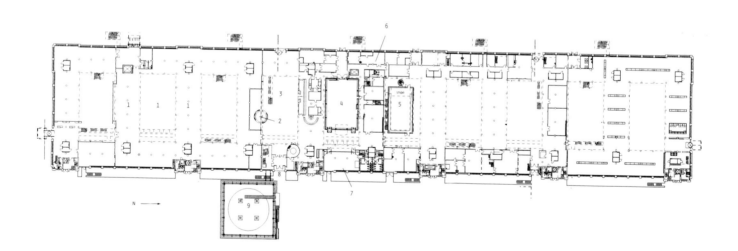

left: The tough industrial structure provides a good context for large-scale art works.

right: The new 'cube' acts as a symbol of renewal – the rather grim past of the complex has now been superseded by a new life.

facing page: One of the inner courtyards, which has been glazed over to form exhibition spaces.

Oxo Tower Wharf LONDON, UK

LIFSCHUTZ DAVIDSON, 1993–96

London's South Bank, close to the City and West End, has long been cut off from the life of the metropolis. The early twentieth-century County Hall, built as the seat of local government and the South Bank Centre developed in the 1960s around the 1951 Royal Festival Hall, all represent attempts to break down that isolation. More recently, the National Theatre has provided a further cultural focus south of the Thames. The river remains, however, a massive divide. The area between Blackfriars and Waterloo bridges was the scene of one of the epic planning battles of post-war London. Attempts to develop the area around Coin Street as a mix of housing, shops and offices came to grief in the 1980s. Richard Rogers' abortive masterplan would have linked the area to the north bank of the river by a new bridge and given it a new urban form focused on Europe's largest glazed galleria. The scheme was defeated by local activists, who insisted that the Coin Street area should remain residential, a place for the 'local community', not outsiders. They were strengthened by the left-wing Greater London Council – soon to be withdrawn – which made over its own landholdings there to the Coin Street Community Association and the area was developed as social housing.

The recycled Oxo Building, together with recent housing also designed by Lifschutz Davidson (a practice formed out of the Richard Rogers office), represents a surprising outcome to the bitter battles of the past. Under the Rogers scheme, the sturdy but unexceptional turn-of-the-century concrete warehouse, together with the tower advertising Oxo meat products added on top (c.1930) would have disappeared. But Coin Street Community Builders (CSCB) (as it had become) saw the potential of the building for reuse. Having abandoned its militantly anti-commercial outlook, CSCB saw the potential for combining commercial and social uses within the same building.

Lifschutz Davidson's brief was to provide rented Housing Association apartments, plus shops and restaurants, and also some rented studios for artists and craftspeople – an element that CSCB was keen to encourage in the area. The building was, in fact, very suited to this approach. Major structural changes were neither practical nor necessary. Three service and access cores were gouged out at the centre and either end of the block. The five floors of apartments were easily accommodated within the existing structure, with access from a central corridor. The fact that the building was unlisted and undervalued made the architects' task easier – in Britain, a rigid and retrograde attitude often prevails towards the reuse of listed buildings. The attachment of steel balconies to the façades, for example, was not contentious. Below the apartments are three floors of working studios and shops, plus an attractive café designed by Apicella Associates. Several years on, the shops have been slow to let. In contrast, the restaurant and brasserie on the top floor of the building (accessed by a lift direct from street and river level) has become one of the most modish eating places in London.

Food apart, the reason was clear: a unique view spanning a vast stretch of the river and the City. The old roof structure was completely removed and replaced by a dynamic new 'wing', under which sit the two eating spaces, kitchens and cloakrooms. After the economical and relatively pragmatic conversion of the other floors, the top floor (let to the modish Harvey Nichols group) provided scope for the imagination. The form of the new roof provides ample head-height, while the immaculately detailed all-glazed façade to the river maximizes views out. (There is an external terrace for fine weather.) The roof structure is both functional and decorative: a system of moveable fins varies daylight levels and allows mood changes by the use of different colours during day and night.

The Oxo development was a daring move, mixing not only uses but social mores – the weekly rent of the apartments is around the price of an average lunch for two in the Harvey Nichols restaurant. The scheme remains to be completed with the conversion of the adjacent Barge House block, linked to the Oxo Building by an open yard (to be covered with a fabric awning and used for performances). It has provided a massive boost for the neglected South Bank and confirms that innovative design and progressive social intentions need not be at odds.

above: A large café on the second floor, designed by Apicella Associates, is a
focal point of the recycled building.
facing page: The top-floor restaurant has a terrace, overlooking the river and
covered by a lightweight glazed canopy.

TEMPORARY CONTEMPORARY MUSEUM LOS ANGELES, USA

FRANK O. GEHRY & ASSOCIATES, 1982–83; 1995–

Over ten years after its completion, the Temporary Contemporary remains an apparently permanent feature of the Los Angeles cultural scene. The idea of a modern art museum as a symbol of regeneration in the city's downtown area emerged in the late 1970s and eventually resulted in Arata Isozaki's Museum of Contemporary Art in 1986. MOCA is set among the big but bland office towers of Bunker Hill. While it was under construction, the Temporary Contemporary, located in LA's Little Tokyo and opened in 1983, staged exhibitions and prepared the ground for the permanent museum.

Gehry described the budget for the scheme as 'absolutely rock-bottom' – around $1 million. (Isozaki's budget was $22 million.) The raw material was a block of empty property – a large warehouse, together with a former police garage and a derelict filling-station, set on a dead-end street. The total area of the buildings amounted to 5,760 square metres (62,000 square feet). As a first step, the buildings had to be repaired and stabilized, with new services and access arrangements – a series of ramps allowed total access for the disabled. Most of the budget went on making the buildings usable. The only obviously 'architectural' intervention was the new external canopy – vital, Gehry judged, since the building faced being islanded by the clearance of the surrounding area and needed to establish a recognizable identity.

'We really did not do that much', Gehry commented. 'We did sweep the floor and clean the skylights and steam-clean the structure and ceiling rather than sandblast it, which I thought was important. We let the character of the old warehouse exist, tried not to change it and thus subordinate it, but rather to work within it to create a flexible space for contemporary art.'

Within the great, uncluttered interior, moveable partitions provided hanging space – nothing was permanent. Indeed, the building provided an excellent venue for performances – a huge stage could easily be accommodated. *Available Light*, a collaboration between Gehry, composer John Adams and choreographer Lucinda Childs staged in 1983, demonstrated its potential in this direction. The Temporary Contemporary was a huge success, with 85,000 visitors in its first three months. Such was its popularity that it did not close when the Isozaki museum opened. It was not closed until 1992, with demolition threatened as developers eyed the valuable site.

In 1995, the Temporary Contemporary reopened and a masterplan to refurbish it for the long term was announced. With Gehry again as architect, new education facilities, a reading room and shop were added. A second phase of renovation focused on the piazza outside the museum, where a bookshop, coffee bar and performance space were added in 1995–96. Finally, a studio/classroom, interactive media space, administrative offices and improved security systems were completed in 1997. The main exhibition space was refurbished and a closer link between the interior and outdoor exhibition spaces was established. With a long lease on the building, the Temporary Contemporary was able to plan its future as a vital element of the West Coast art scene.

The Temporary Contemporary was a pioneering project, encouraging Angelenos to look at the huge resource of redundant industrial and warehouse spaces in the city and to envisage them recycled as places to live and work. (Gehry's own office was in a recycled warehouse, while he lived in a restyled but still typical suburban house in Santa Monica.) It was Gehry who discovered the potential of a recent, but still valuable, built heritage and made the city of Los Angeles recognize the value of reuse.

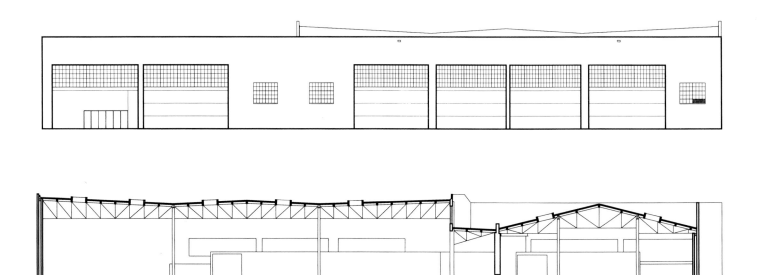

above: Elevation and cross-section.

facing page: Gehry left the lofty and simple internal space much as found, resulting

in a flexible space for contemporary art.

AGRONOMIC FACULTY GEMBLOUX, BELGIUM

SAMYN AND PARTNERS ARCHITECTS AND ENGINEERS, 1993–95

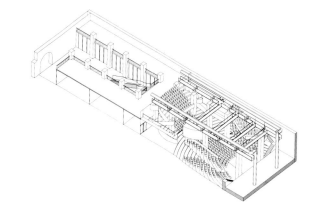

facing page: The new auditorium at Gembloux sits comfortably within the great volume of an old barn – the brick piers and timber roof form the architectural setting.
right: Axonometric view.

Historic barns, often monumental in scale and among the most striking monuments produced by the agrarian societies of the past, pose a major conservation problem in many European countries and in parts of North America. (William Morris extolled the barn at Great Coxwell, Berkshire, as being 'grand as a cathedral'.) Many have been lost, others spoiled by insensitive conversions – residential use is common but is, in fact, generally inappropriate, since it involves breaking up a whole into a number of small spaces. Public and commercial uses can often preserve at least something of the internal character of a barn.

The Agronomic Faculty at Gembloux is housed in a secularized medieval abbey. The acquisition of a nearby listed farm complex allowed the University of Gembloux to create an auditorium (also used as a conference hall and venue for concerts and drama) in the great barn of the farm, completed in 1762. A competition for the conversion was won by Brussels-based Samyn and Partners and provided for a 600-seat auditorium plus a number of smaller lecture and conference rooms.

The listed status of the barn predicated a minimal intervention. (The architects worked closely with Belgium's *Commission Royale des Monuments et des Sites* throughout.) The integrity of the historic structure – 11 brick piers on each side, supporting a magnificent timber roof – had to be respected. But the subdivision of the internal volume was inevitable: half was allotted to the auditorium, the remainder to the foyer and other ancillary spaces. New galleries and the mezzanines that provide access to them are distinctively contemporary in feel. Staircases formed in steel and timber provide essential fire and emergency escape routes. The new auditorium is a warm and intimate space, with very good sight lines.

The aesthetic of the transformation is entirely modern but intended to be almost 'rustic' in its emphasis on function – services are frankly but unselfconsciously exposed. Timber is used extensively, for example for the new auditorium seating. New floors are of brick or stone. Existing brick and stonework has been repaired, repointed and cleaned up. Timber beams have been left as found, though reinforced with steel. Air-conditioning was not necessary, given the nature of the structure and the effectiveness of cross-ventilation. Acoustic panels have been inconspicuously installed at roof level, providing acoustic conditions suitable for music or the spoken word.

The Gembloux project impresses by its rigorous, but completely undemonstrative, commitment to the character of the existing building. Its chief merit lies, however, in the creation of distinctive new spaces within the context of a larger existing volume. The most significant element was probably the restraint shown by a client determined to achieve a dignified transformation rather than utilize space to the maximum.

133

NATIONAL STUDIO FOR CONTEMPORARY ARTS LE FRESNOY, LILLE, FRANCE

BERNARD TSCHUMI ARCHITECTS, 1991–98

The buildings that form the core of this remarkable – indeed, definitive – project of transformation were once a focus of local community life. The site at Le Fresnoy, in the industrial suburbs of Lille, was developed in the 1900s as a workers' playground, with dance halls, bars, cafés and a roller-skating rink. A 1,000-seat cinema was soon added. On Sundays and national holidays, crowds came to relax there. In the early 1970s, however, after years of decline, the complex was suddenly closed down and stood empty for 15 years, slowly decaying. According to Alain Fleischer, founding director of the National Studio, the existence of the old buildings was critical in the development of the project – 'the discovery of this abandoned ship, still ringing with the echoes of its past, not only provided the idea of installing the project on this site but also became the concrete manifestation of the project'.

The National Studio is a pioneering post-graduate school for film and visual arts, funded by central, regional (Nord/Pas de Calais) and local governments. Fleischer was committed to northern France and initially envisaged a redundant industrial building as a possible base for the new institution. The Le Fresnoy buildings were discovered by chance in 1987.

An architectural competition for the development of the site was organized in 1991 and won by Tschumi, who proposed to repair and reuse the existing buildings, while sheltering them beneath a reconstructed overall roof carrying all new services. Work on site began in 1994, with the first students admitted towards the end of 1997. The most fruitful comparisons of Tschumi's scheme can be made, perhaps, with the work of Eric Owen Moss at Culver City (pages 88–95). But, whereas Moss's work is about intervention, insertion and perpetual contrast, Tschumi envelopes the old work within a new whole, creating a fresh unity. The retention of most of the existing buildings as 'boxes' within the revised envelope made obvious practical sense, since a wide variety of spaces was required for teaching and performance use. As Tschumi remarked, comparing the academies of the present age with the more clearly defined disciplines of the Bauhaus:

> We were not dealing with coherent, well-defined disciplines... but with the disparate multiplicity of performance art, cinema, video and film production, sound studios, a school, a restaurant, several exhibition areas and industrial facilities for multimedia crafts... We decided to play the site's inherent complexity through contemporary concepts.

For Tschumi, the 'in between' space, above the old buildings and below the new roof, is the key to the scheme:

> This immense horizontal space questions the notions of interior and exterior suggested by the old buildings. Such multi-functional spaces will be the urban spaces of the twenty-first century.

The new space is not so much an object as an 'event'. It is a place for interaction: Le Fresnoy is a public place, as well as an academy, with a regional film theatre and a regular exhibition programme. It is essentially open to the outside world and accessible to all, in theory, via a network of walkways and platforms – though the infirm and cautious may find this upper-level realm rather intimidating. For most, though, it is a benign, radiant, and above all, an inspirational inside-out space, executed with enormous verve and contempt for the merely rational; a giant sculptural umbrella with the impact of a football stadium rising over the mundane brick terraces. Le Fresnoy has challenged every conventional idea of reuse and established a new/old dialogue which is entirely contemporary.

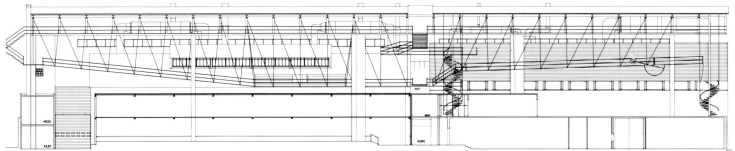

Longitudinal section.

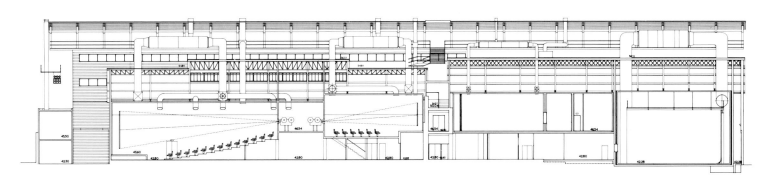

Cross-section showing cinemas, sound studios and the film set.

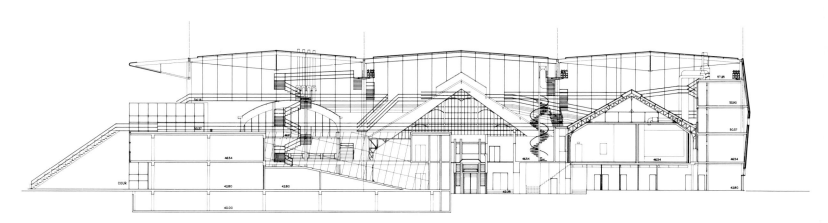

South-north section showing the new roof enveloping the existing buildings.

facing page: The new container sits comfortably on top of the old buildings – quite utilitarian sheds – and provides a zone for servicing and circulation.

following page: The new structure has a powerful, even dominating presence amid the streets of brick-built workers' housing – rather like a football stadium.

CITIZENS' ART CENTRE KANAZAWA, JAPAN

ICHIRO MIZUNO AND KANAZAWA PLANNING RESEARCH COMPANY, 1995–96

The Kanazawa Citizens' Art Centre is a pioneering project, in Japanese terms, transforming an old warehouse complex into an arts centre.

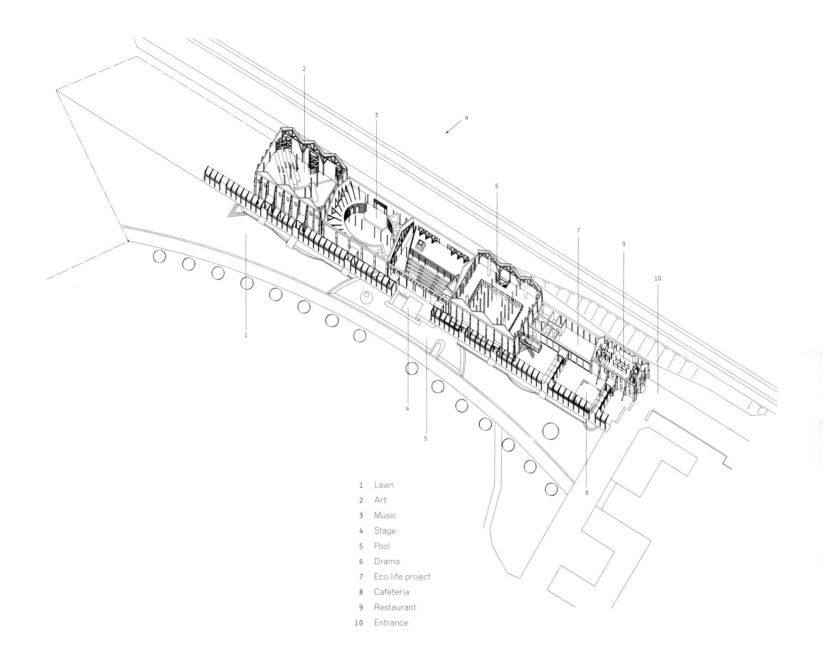

1 Lawn
2 Art
3 Music
4 Stage
5 Pool
6 Drama
7 Eco-life project
8 Cafeteria
9 Restaurant
10 Entrance

N

The Kanazawa Citizens' Art Centre is housed in a group of factory buildings dating from the 1920s and 1930s, structures of brick with timber and reinforced concrete that possess resource value rather than great historic interest.

The intention behind the transformation project was to provide an umbrella for a number of cultural activities in the city – theatre, music, video, art exhibitions and even ecological projects were catered for. Within the tough framework of the old buildings, a series of adaptable spaces were created. New interventions take their cue from the existing buildings and the emphasis is on durability and flexibility. Spaces are in use around the clock, and the centre has become a major local landmark.

143

above: The renovation has preserved the existing structure – new interventions do not compromise the impressive spaces.

facing page: The theatre: its simplicity recalls traditional Japanese architecture.

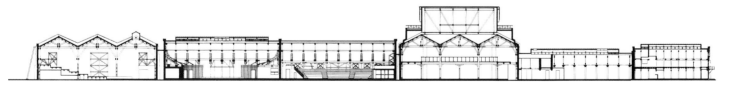

Cross-section showing the linear layout of the buildings.

DUTCH DESIGN INSTITUTE AMSTERDAM, THE NETHERLANDS

BENTHEM CROUWEL ARCHITEKTEN, 1992–94

The reconstruction of a nineteenth-century building on the Keizersgracht (the very core of historic, touristic Amsterdam) as a centre for new design, has all the rigour that might be expected from one of the most dynamic modern practices in the Netherlands. The former Fodor Museum had been built in the 1860s, funded by coal magnate and collector Carl Fodor and designed by Cornelis Oudshoorn. The museum, that extended into two adjacent houses, closed some years ago, and the canalside buildings deteriorated with disuse. Their physical condition was so poor that the conversion scheme undertaken by Benthem Crouwel had to begin with the reinforcement of foundations, partial reconstruction of façades, strengthening of floors and replacement of rotting window-frames. The total reconstruction of the existing fabric reflected the complete transformation of use: from preserving works of art to documenting the design of everyday manufactured objects. The interiors were considered largely expendable, though anything of historic interest, such as chimney pieces, was kept. The exterior had to remain unchanged in its canal aspect: changes to the rear elevation were acceptable.

Benthem Crouwel re-thought the format of the buildings in line with ideas developed by the director of the new Institute, John Thackara, who saw the building as a 'think-and-do-tank' that needed to reflect a dynamic design philosophy. The collecting and documenting role of the Institute was tackled by erecting a new structure, nicknamed the 'collector', within a lightwell carved out of the rear of the old houses. The 'collector' allows the whole of the building to be kept free of cupboards and cases and displays items from the collection in a very uncluttered fashion. Ten metres (33 feet) high, this translucent steel and glass arrangement concentrates what is often untidily and inconveniently dispersed by containing book stacks, paper archives, objects and computer technology. Within the 1860s block, a new staircase, suspended from the roof and daylit from above, with bridges paved in blue glass slabs, connects all existing floors. (Old buildings in Amsterdam are inevitably vertical in character, but a new lift serves those unable to use the stairs.) A staircase designed by Mart Stam in 1954 was removed.

The architects were closely involved in the design of furniture and fittings. Walls are white and floors are generally restored nineteenth-century parquet. Large wooden tables temper the impact of glass and steel, but the general effect is one of transparency and lightness. Natural light is particularly well used in what was originally a confined and dark site. In a small space, Benthem Crouwel have demonstrated how a few bold moves can transform what seemed a very unpromising location for a radical new institution.

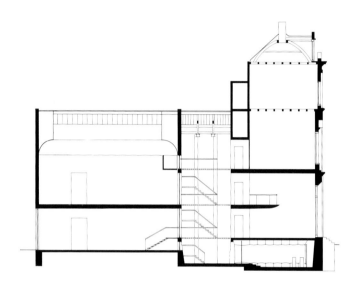

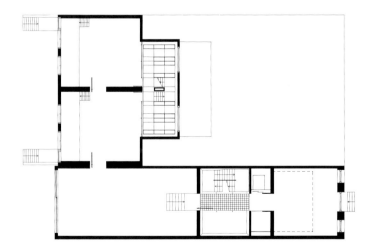

facing page: Old and new are rigorously counterpoised to create a dynamic
architectural effect and to meet new practical needs.
above: Section and ground-floor plan.

LA LLAUNA SCHOOL BADALONA, BARCELONA, SPAIN

ENRIC MIRALLES BENEDETTA TAGLIABUE ARQUITECTES ASSOCIATS WITH CARME PINÓS, 1984–86; 1993–94

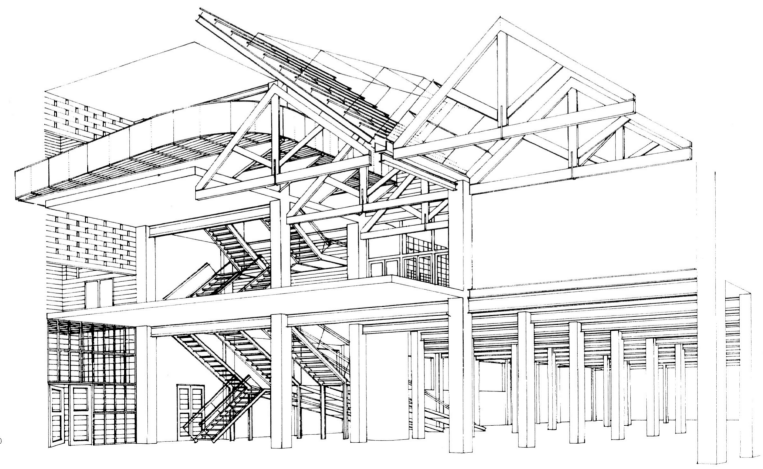

Within the container of an old factory in Barcelona, Miralles and Pinós have inserted the working and

circulation spaces of a modern school – stairs and ramps ascend within a formerly open space.

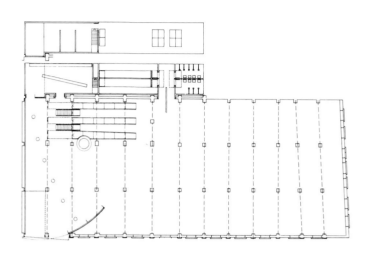

Ground-floor plan

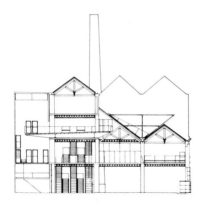

Cross-section

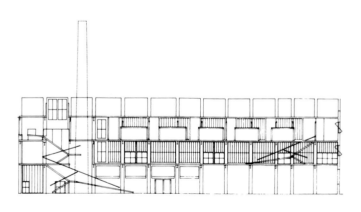

Section showing the main staircase

Miralles and Pinós's transformation of a redundant factory into a secondary school is simultaneously one of the most pragmatic and yet the most poetic of their earlier projects. (Most of the scheme was executed between 1984–86: the second phase involved the remodelling of the ground floor and entrance area.) The starting point was the existing building, a big-boned industrial structure in an old factory quarter, where the streets provide little space for children. An over-cautious conversion of the old factory would have reinforced the feeling of enclosure and constraint. Instead, the architects were 'to explode the constraining context and to set in place a counter-statement around such themes as interpenetration, illumination, and social openness'. A key strategy was the vertical opening of the interiors to allow natural light to pervade the new spaces. Staircases and ramps link the floors and offer a zone for socializing, as well as for circulation. Externally, new openings in the heavy masonry walls 'announces a modernization and change of use in the premises... [and] suggests accessibility, transparency and diagonality'. These themes pervade the renewed interior of the building. The focus of the school is the covered playground on the ground floor, an 'inside/outside' space which is the starting point for a series of routes through the building. The aim was to make these routes clear and direct: the corridors are wide enough to be meeting places. (Miralles links the idea of 'building as street' to the theories of Team X and the Smithsons, whose Hunstanton School, constructed between 1949–54, precisely embodied this concept.) The notion of school and street overlapping was important to the whole project.

Miralles and Pinós's second phase, however, modifies the concept to some degree. Increased security was required, along with storage for bicycles and this has been achieved without compromising the character of the building. Miralles believes that the 'confusion between what the building is today and what it was' is part of its appeal – it has been popular with users and with critics. 'The layout and the new construction are closely linked to the old building to the point of being confused with it', Miralles has written. '"New" and "old" no longer exist – just a different way of playing in the interior of the building.'

above: New spaces are constructed within the framework of the old structure.

facing page: The new staircases are deliberately dramatized as a focus for the transformed interior and provide a natural place for socializing.

TRUST THEATRE AMSTERDAM, THE NETHERLANDS

MECANOO ARCHITEKTEN, 1995–96

left: Externally, the building remains unchanged; its elegant eighteenth-century façade has been carefully restored.

facing page: The conversion of a redundant church in Amsterdam into a theatre necessitated new access and service facilities – which were concentrated within a freestanding 'box'.

More than any other building type, churches pose complex problems of conversion and reuse. The problems are not only physical – it is generally unacceptable to subdivide the interiors of historic churches – but equally philosophical and even theological. Churches are public buildings and to annex them for entirely private uses is usually inappropriate. In the Catholic tradition, the act of consecration sets a church apart from 'worldly' use. Certain activities such as bars or nightclubs may seem irreverent. 'Cultural' uses such as concert halls, libraries and theatres are, however, generally acceptable to all denominations.

In the Protestant tradition, no special quality of the sacred or numinous applies to church buildings. When the Evangelical Lutheran church at Kloveniersburgwal in Amsterdam (dating from the 1790s) closed in 1952, the building was sold to the Nederlandsche Bank, which used it for 30 years as an archive store. The form of the building – a straightforward aisled rectangle with little obviously ecclesiastical imagery – adapted well enough to this mundane use. Such fittings as existed were disposed of: the large and fine organ went to a church in Arnhem. The internal space was lost under banks of files. Eventually, the bank moved out. Lacking a use, the building gradually headed towards complete dereliction.

Salvation came with the De Trust theatre company, a fringe group seeking a permanent base. The company did not have a massive budget and converting an existing building was a virtually inevitable course. In any case, the informal and adaptable character of old buildings was in tune with its outlook. The Trust Theatre likes the idea that it is a 'guest' in the building and may one day move on: it did not want to be dominated by the structure nor permanently rooted to it. But it did want to provide good amenities for both performers and audiences.

Mecanoo's proposal was in line with this philosophy. The approach was to make each new intervention genuinely reversible: old and new are kept distinct, so that the quality of both can be appreciated. But the driving force behind the project was to create an effective and practical theatre. The main auditorium sits within the former worship space at first-floor level. The seating is within a freestanding raked structure extending up to gallery level. The 'stage' is at floor level – the essence of De Trust's approach is flexible and ad hoc and a fixed stage was not required. The gallery level has been infilled – new partitions stand well back from the elegant timber columns – to provide dressing rooms and offices as well as a spacious rehearsal room. Foyer space and lavatories are accommodated at ground-floor level.

Access (and escape) requirements were greatly intensified with the change of use. Rather than cut new staircases through the fabric, the architects hit on the ingenious idea of installing a massive piece of 'furniture' in the space left vacant by the removed organ. The new staircase to the theatre is contained within this structure, as are the bar and kitchen and, at upper level, the technical controls box. In theory, this intervention could be relatively easily stripped out. If the church were to be used for worship again, a new organ could fit into the space.

A particularly successful aspect of the scheme is its use of strong colour, dignified but rich and inviting. Warm red and ochre hues, together with the texture of cleaned and waxed natural timber, mitigate the effect of the austere new detailing. The building has a strong atmosphere, not that of a conventional theatre but making excellent use of natural light. Mecanoo's lean modernism seems to be in the same spirit as the austere but joyful architecture of the Lutheran tradition. The marriage of the two has produced a new stimulus to the perennial debate on the problem of surplus churches.

below: Old and new architecture are boldly juxtaposed in the transformed interior and there is a strong emphasis on the contrasted materials.
facing page: The new auditorium is a freestanding element within the church – it can be totally removed should the building's use change again.

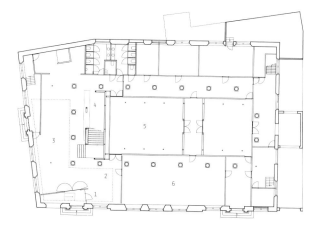

Ground-floor plan

1   Entrance
2   Cash desk
3   Foyer
4   Bar
5   Small auditorium
6   Offices

PERFORMANCE SPACE MARAIS, PARIS, FRANCE

CUNO BRULLMANN S.A. D'ARCHITECTURE, 1991-92

facing page: The former Marché des Blancs Manteaux in Paris's Marais district, early nineteenth century in date but with a later steel roof, has been converted to a multi-purpose performance space.

Before launching his own practice, Swiss-born Brullmann spent five formative years with Piano and Rogers, working on the Pompidou Centre. Consequently, his architecture shares the rich and accretive approach of his mentors and their interest in the interface of old and new. Brullmann's other conversion schemes include the transformation of a nineteenth-century commercial block into offices for Paris's city architects (1986–88) and of a factory at Aubergenville into a training centre (1989–90).

The 1,000 square-metre (10,764 square-foot) Blancs Manteaux market stands in the heart of the Marais, east of the Pompidou Centre, and dates from the early nineteenth century. Externally, it is clad in ashlar, with classical details. The interior roof was originally of timber, but after a fire early this century, it was rebuilt in steel, in a particularly elegant form. The market had gone through several changes of use before the present scheme, with little respect shown to the historic fabric: the interior was subdivided, mezzanines introduced at various points and original openings blocked. Part of the roof had actually been removed. The value of the building was perceived only when the Marais itself was reprieved from threats of clearance and systematically regenerated.

The initiative to restore the old market came from the City of Paris, with plans to create a flexible theatre/performance space serving the local community. Brullmann's project combined restoration and innovative new design. The lost section of the roof was rebuilt in replica. The project was based on a commitment to conserve the internal space, cleared of later intrusions. Fixed seating was not provided, due to the building's possible future use as a covered sports facility and/or a venue for performing dance. Lavatories, changing rooms, administrative offices and other services are placed in enclosed spaces at the corners. These interventions are in a contrasting style, the aim being to evoke the idea of a building within a building. From the street, there is a view through a fully glazed arch into the open interior. What was a minor incident in the rich townscape of the Marais has become a visual highlight.

above: An arch to the street, formerly filled by heavy gates, has been glazed to provide views in and out of the building.

facing page: New interventions are designed in an entirely modern manner.

LUDWIG FORUM FOR INTERNATIONAL ART AACHEN, GERMANY

ELLER + ELLER ARCHITEKTEN, 1988–91

above: Josef Bachmann's umbrella factory of 1927–28 was a good example of the rational industrial architecture of the period.
facing page: The generous daylight provision of the existing building enhanced its potential for reuse.

Fritz Eller's conversion of a former umbrella factory into the home of the Ludwig Forum – containing a part of the remarkable art collection of Peter and Irene Ludwig – is exemplary for its respectful (rather than reverential) approach to an existing building dating from modernism's classic period.

The Ludwigs began collecting in the early 1950s. Irene Ludwig was a native of Aachen, one of Germany's most historic cities: in 1968 their collection of American pop art, then little known in Europe, was shown in the city. The lack of a suitable local venue for a permanent exhibition led, however, to the Ludwigs making a major donation to the Wallraf-Richartz Museum in Cologne. Aachen lost out.

The opening two years later, however, of a new gallery in Aachen's restored *Kurhaus* (assembly rooms) allowed parts of the collection to be put on semi-permanent display. In many respects, though, not least its period ambience, the *Kurhaus* was at odds with the art. In the mid-1980s, the city resolved to commit public funds to a permanent home for the Ludwigs' collection, seeing it as a twentieth-century addition to a patrimony extending back to the Romans.

The former umbrella factory (capable of turning out 10,000 umbrellas a day) on Aachen's Jülicher Strasse, within walking distance of the historic city centre, had recently closed. It was in sound condition and was clearly in need of a suitable use. Its architectural quality was indisputable. Designed by Josef Bachmann and constructed in 1927–28, it was a model of modernist rationalism in the Bauhaus tradition.

Most of the building consisted of a lofty, single-storey, toplit production space, fronted by a three-storey office wing. It offered up to 6,000 square metres

(64,583 square feet) of potential display space, plus all the additional amenities of a modern museum. But the conversion was to be more than just a museum – flats and studios to be rented to artists were planned. The Forum was to present art 'not as a result but as an experience'. The raw industrial quality of the former factory was considered highly appropriate to this philosophy and the aim was to preserve the ambience of a factory, not a museum.

Externally, the scope for change was limited – new signage denoted the change of use. Inside the building, an area 15 x 15 metres (49 x 49 feet) at the centre of the production floor was excavated as a performance space for events such as music and dance. This large internal space (there are no corridors) proved ideal for showing sculpture – an important part of the collection – although enclosed, light-controlled galleries have been created for pictures and graphic works. Lecture rooms, as well as a bookshop and café were also provided. Four corner 'towers' contain the ancillary functions – library, administrative offices and sculpture studios. A sizeable area of land attached to the factory was used to create a sculpture park, as well as a parking area. An open loggia provides an 'inside-out' space for display or events. The coincidence of a vacant building with a perceived need was fortuitous. But the conversion has a lightness of touch that makes the union of the two seem inevitable.

Ground-floor plan

1	Sculpture courtyard	8	Storeroom
2	Workroom	9	Painting gallery
3	Information	10	Library
4	Bookshop	11	Painting gallery
5	Sculpture gallery	12	Cafeteria/bar
6	Archive	13	Entrance to artist's flat
7	Darkroom		

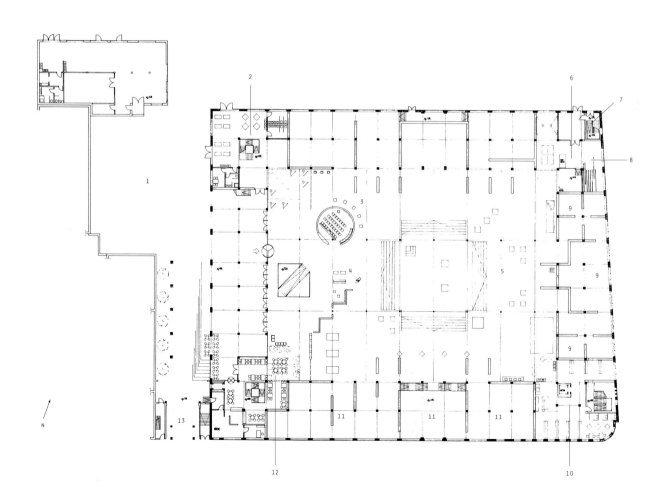

The conversion of the internal space is free of gimmicks – it provided the flexibility that
the new users needed. A sunken performance area is the main innovation.

FLOAT MUSEUM JOHANA, TOYAMA PREFECTURE, JAPAN

BENSON + FORSYTH WITH SUZUKI ARCHITECTS OFFICE, 1992–93

left: Benson + Forsyth's transformation of a group of timber warehouses into a museum juxtaposed old fabric with new interventions of glass and steel.
right: A new extension to the complex brings light into the whole interior and includes a new circulation route.

This new museum, focusing on local identity, is intended as a major addition to the cultural amenities of the Toyama Prefecture – an area of striking natural beauty – and as part of a programme encouraging the towns in the region to develop new museums and arts centres. The programme was coordinated by Arata Isozaki Architects, who were encouraged to recruit foreign architects for a number of the commissions.

At Johana, a project which transformed existing buildings (wooden warehouses) rather than creating a new building, was chosen. Benson + Forsyth worked in association with a Tokyo practice and in close consultation with the local committee promoting the scheme. Johana is an ancient town, with strong roots in the silk industry and in woodworking. The ornately carved and decorated floats used in religious festivals over the centuries reflect the skills of local craftsmen and have been preserved in a museum in the centre of the town, next to the historic Zentoku-ji Temple. The new museum provides an improved setting for the display of these historic artefacts. The four storehouses housing the museum are a prominent landmark and were acquired by the local authority some

years ago and maintained pending an appropriate new use. The transformation scheme brought together traditional Japanese wooden construction and the ideas of a Western practice with roots in the Modern Movement, yet the interaction of the two worked well. Alterations and additions were kept to a minimum, and were essentially links between the existing buildings to allow their use as one continuing structure. Benson + Forsyth commented that 'the Japanese tradition of heavy roof and light screen walls is inverted. The wall of the galleria, although lightweight in terms of fabric, has a thickness which contains stairs, niches and is "inhabited". The roof is a glazed screen of overlaid, structural glazing and louvre grids.' To the street, the appearance of the old warehouses is unchanged. To the garden side, however, a radical new extension transforms the ensemble. The interior, with clearly articulated columns and beams carrying a new structure of steel and glass, makes obvious reference to the Japanese building tradition.

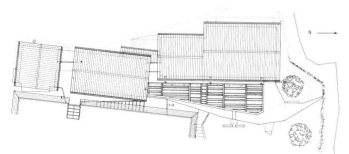

left: Roof plan.

above: The new extension is a stark contrast, in form and materials, to the historic building.

EUROPEAN HOUSE OF PHOTOGRAPHY MARAIS, PARIS, FRANCE

YVES LION ARCHITECTE, 1990–96

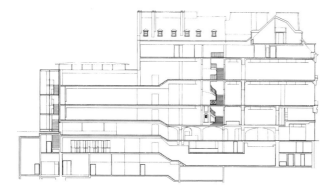

left: Section through the building showing the meeting of the new and old structures.
facing page: Yves Lion's new addition is stylistically far removed from the adjacent *hôtel particulier* but is carefully designed to echo its scale and materials.
following page: The project has opened up a new garden and a view of the historic building formerly blocked by later additions.

The Hôtel Hénault de Cantobre on the edge of the regenerated Marais was a 'problem' building before its conversion into a photographic museum funded by the City of Paris. The Marais had once had a number of rundown and threatened *hôtels particuliers* (private mansions), mostly seventeenth and eighteenth century in date: new, largely cultural, uses have been their salvation.

The eighteenth-century Hôtel Hénault de Cantobre, long subdivided into substandard apartments and partly used for industrial purposes, now occupies a site on the corner of the rue François Miron and the rue de Fourcy, close to the rue de Rivoli. As it is a protected *monument historique*, any significant changes to its structure and appearance were ruled out. However, the demolition of a later, derelict building that blocked out views of the *hôtel* from the rue de Fourcy was permitted and there were plans to replace this with a new building. It was clear that an extension would be needed to accommodate all the uses envisaged – library, bookshop and cinema – even with all available space used in the old building. (In the refurbished structure, the attics are given over to offices.)

Yves Lion – the son of a professional photographer – won the job in competition in 1990. Construction began in March 1993, and the new institution opened early in 1996. Work to the protected monument was limited to restoration, in accordance with the stipulations of the *Bâtiments de France*. However, a new building was attached to the rear wing of the old building, accessed by a covered way from the street. The title 'house' of photography had some significance – there was a clear attempt to retain a sense of intimacy and comfort, of discovery and delight, rather than to impose a formally didactic museological aura. The diverse spaces within the old building were seen as a resource and a similar ambience was sought from the new interiors. Lion's building seems quite modest from outside: the four storeys clearly defer to its historic neighbour. In fact, two very large spaces, the library (partly naturally lit via a deep slot in the entrance

foyer) and auditorium, along with stores and workshops, are contained at basement level below the entrance court, where there are links to the refurbished cellars of the *hôtel*.

One of the refreshing features of the new building is its irregularity and unpredictability. Effortlessly, it seems, Lion has responded to the historic context, creating a series of flowing spaces in what seems, superficially, a rectangular and highly rational structure. Use of stone similar to that of the *hôtel* as a facing material binds the two structures together, while the insertion of a vertical band of sheer glazing helps avoid an abrupt join. The question of scale, Lion says, was critical to the whole project. The new building had to be discreet but not so discreet that it could be ignored. Old and new must 'co-habit'. The best of new work, he says, increases the stature of the old, but without condescension. Old buildings equally enrich the context of new ones. A note of dissent from the general welcome given to the completed project came from critic Jean-Paul Robert, who argued that the old *hôtels particuliers* should be lived in again, not sold out to the 'culture industry' promoted by the city authorities at the expense of the living city. Robert's point is valid. Old buildings adapt well to new uses: the rooms of the Hôtel Hénault de Cantobre make fine galleries. But could Lion's galleries, library and cinema ever be lived in? The issue may never arise. For the moment, Lion's beautifully made addition to the Marais is there to be celebrated and enjoyed.

above: There are views out from the new gallery space to the historic street beyond.

facing page: Old and new buildings are unobtrusively linked.

HAKODATE BAY REGENERATION HOKKAIDO, JAPAN

OKADA & ASSOCIATES/ARCHITECTS ENGINEERS PLANNERS, 1988

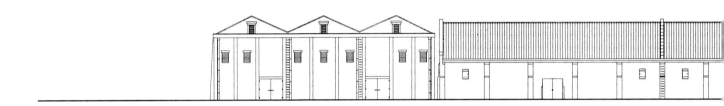

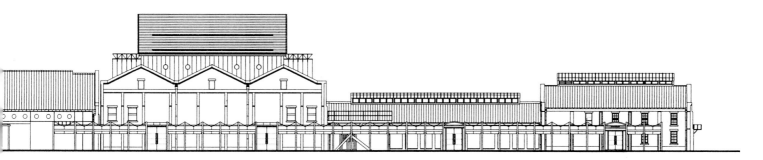

above: West elevation before and after renovation.

following page: The Hakodate Bay project has given life to a group of waterside warehouses, recycled for retail and leisure uses and linked by a new footbridge across the dock.

The regeneration of the old port area of Hakodate, the largest conurbation in the northern Japanese island of Hokkaido, involved the imaginative conversion of a group of historic buildings. In the context of the Japanese architectural and development scene, the project was highly innovative.

The port of Hakodate contains a number of warehouses dating from the period 1880 to 1910, when the city – still rich in nineteenth-century architecture – developed rapidly. Mostly comprising one or two storeys, the warehouses are constructed of brick with timber or steel roof structures and had obvious conversion potential.

Working with the Shimizu Corporation, architects Okada & Associates drew up a strategy for the site. Some demolition was carried out to allow access and parking and to create open, waterside space – in Hakodate, like many other great ports, the waterfront was largely inaccessible to the public. Two warehouses,

both around 1,800 square metres (19,375 square feet) in size and located along two sides of a canal, were transformed into a development of shops, bars and restaurants. The architectural approach was eclectic, including both restoration of the existing fabric and radical new interventions, though the aim was to preserve the industrial aesthetic of the buildings. A lightweight canal footbridge was constructed to connect the two warehouses, one of which was partially unroofed to create an external, enclosed piazza. A short distance away, another group of warehouses has become the Hakodate History Plaza, which accommodates conference and restaurant facilities as well as shops.

Along with the conversion of other buildings in the port area – for example, the former British Consulate – these projects, clearly inspired by the success of waterfront regenerations in the USA, have made Hakodate a pioneer in the field of reuse and transformation.

CHAPTER 3
MUSEUMS TRANSFORMED

More than 600 new art museums have opened in the USA since 1970. Throughout the world, museums have become the symbols of national and civic pride and indicators of social and economic, as well as cultural, vitality. If the museum was once seen as a repository of history, it is now perceived as a pointer to the future. First conceived as private places for the entertainment of an elite, museums emerged during the Enlightenment as centres for educating the masses – Paris's Louvre and London's British Museum (both the subject of massive late twentieth-century reconstruction schemes) were founded in this spirit.

Renzo Piano and Richard Rogers' Pompidou Centre in Paris, opened in 1977, was forged out of a new ethos in which entertainment was seen as a legitimate aim alongside education. Challenging accepted ways of thinking, rather than reinforcing them, was promoted as a positive aim. The Pompidou aimed to be a vital part of the city, rather than a sanctum set apart – people were allowed, even encouraged, to enjoy the building for its own sake. The idea of the museum as a secular shrine, promulgating a set of accepted doctrines, is today being seriously challenged. The architecture of new museums reflects their changing role. The Saatchi Gallery in London (by Max Gordon Associates) – a former garage – revolutionized the new art scene in Britain in the mid 1980s. Its ad hoc converted premises did not elevate art or set it on a pedestal, but invited people to view it in an open-minded and questioning way. The neutrality of the backcloth was important in the success of the gallery.

In the USA, a programme launched by the federal government in the 1970s set out to provide a series of 'alternative spaces' for art, spaces closer in character to those in which many works of art were created than to traditional museum galleries. Frank Gehry's Temporary Contemporary in Los Angeles drew on the experience of these venues so successfully that it became a permanent venue. Entirely new museums continue to proliferate as a response to the continuing demand for civic monuments. Yet the museum of the future is likely to be less a 'sacred' space than an accessible and friendly placé. The Chinati Foundation at Marfa, Texas, founded by the late Donald Judd, colonized the buildings, most of them entirely utilitarian sheds and hangars, of a former military base. Though Marfa is a remote place, it is an exemplar that has influenced other projects for museums in recycled buildings including Herzog & de Meuron's monumental conversion of Bankside power station in London into the Tate Gallery of Modern Art. Simple, rugged industrial and commercial spaces form an excellent backdrop for works of art and Bankside is not being sanitized for its new use. A more radical approach has, however, been taken by Norman Foster at Essen (pages 182–187), where much of the innards of a former pit engine house

have been retained as a setting for a display of new German design. The appeal of the industrial aesthetic is even reflected in some new purpose-built museum buildings including Gwathmey Siegel's shed-like art museum in Miami (completed in 1996). What Douglas Davis has called 'the non-style style' of museum design has 'flourished at the two extremes of museum management – in low-cost, artist-managed alternative spaces and in gilded institutions created and managed by a single collector'.[1] The challenge posed by transformed buildings to traditional images of the museum is exemplified by sculptor Richard Long's use of a huge aircraft hangar on the outskirts of Palermo for an exhibition created specifically as a response to the space. Building and art are inseparably linked and the idea of the building as passive container – or, worse, an overbearing presence – is refuted. The great Italian collector Guiseppe Panza encouraged the use of former industrial buildings for the display of his huge collection of environmental sculpture – which could not be accommodated in conventional museum galleries. Among the spaces he utilized were the former mills in North Adams, now being converted into the Massachusetts Museum of Contemporary Art.

If a new museum building can eclipse the objects it is intended to display – a betrayal of its purpose, it might be argued – old buildings can equally become exhibits in their own right. In the hands of a few great architects, existing structures of great intrinsic interest have been transformed not only functionally but in terms of their imagery – Scarpa's Castelvecchio at Verona and Stirling's Tate Gallery in Liverpool (since altered) are prominent examples. Forceful buildings created for a specific, now defunct, use make demands on the architect's imagination that match or exceed those posed by new buildings.

1. D. Davis, *The Museum Transformed*, New York 1990, p.182

GERMAN DESIGN CENTRE ESSEN, GERMANY

FOSTER AND PARTNERS, 1994–97

facing page: The boiler house (completed in 1932) at the massive Zollverein XII mine, is a true 'cathedral of power' and formed a natural focus for the regeneration of the abandoned mining site.

following page: The success of Norman Foster's transformation project lies in its acceptance of the existing character of the building and in the balance of old and new elements.

Foster and Partners' German Design Centre, created within the imposing shell of an old colliery power plant, is remarkable for its treatment of the existing fabric, which has been retained as the practical and symbolic framework for a respectful but dynamic intervention. The centre is housed within the huge boiler house of the Zollverein XII mine, developed between the wars into one of the largest and most modern mines in Germany.

The boiler house was the work of architects Fritz Schupp and Martin Kremmer and was completed in 1932. A 'cathedral of power', like London's Battersea and Bankside power stations, the building made good use of the streamlined brickwork of the Dudok style, attached to a steel frame. The mine closed in 1986, one of many closed in the region, but the pithead buildings were considered worthy of retention and reuse and were indeed protected buildings. The recycled boiler house is the focus of the regeneration project for the Zollverein site. The most obvious change to the exterior of the building was the demolition of the tall chimney: this was declared as unsafe before the Foster team was commissioned.

The new centre (opened in May 1997) was intended as part of the regeneration programme for the Ruhr, providing space to display new products and to encourage innovative design. Most of the space inside the building was filled by five enormous boilers, four of which were removed, the last being retained as a poignant relic of the steam age. The spaces that had contained the boilers were, however, kept and reused as exhibition spaces – the essence of the scheme was to live with the interior as found, rather than to radically recast it. (New offices were constructed out of site on top of the building.) The main space has been left undivided to full height – new structures float within the space and are constructed in lightweight materials, with lavish use of glass to ensure maximum transparency. The contrast between the sleek, smooth look of the new work and the worn and battered relics of industry is very deliberate. The new walkways, 40 metres (131 feet) in the air, cut across the upper levels of the interior and provide a new perspective on the industrial past.

The dramatic nature of the scheme is intensified by the approach taken to the display of artefacts: new consumer objects are hung in space or transposed against a background of rusty metal and there is an almost Ruskinian avoidance of 'restoration'. The old work, which was simply repaired and made good where necessary, is celebrated and respected, and gains, rather than loses, from juxtaposition with the new. It is the extraordinary scale and toughness of the old building which contributes most to the success of this scheme, but the delicacy and refinement of the new architecture provides the element of contrast needed to highlight the character of its setting.

183

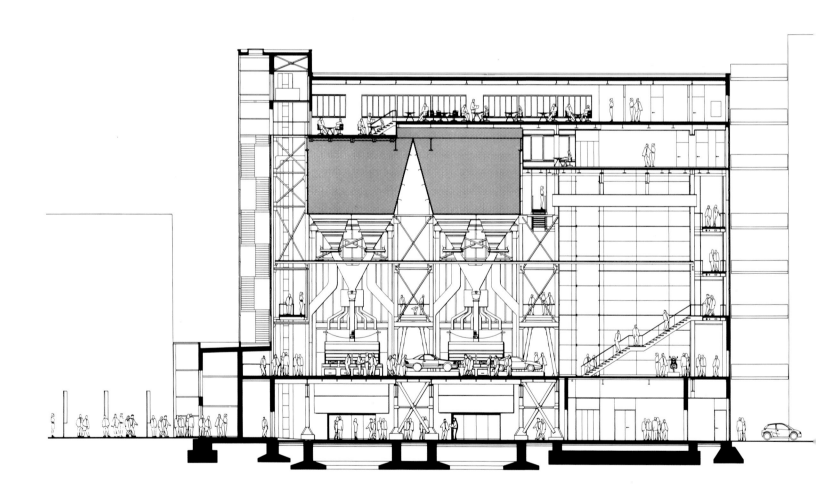

above: Section showing the retained boiler fronts and the way in which new routes have been threaded through the existing industrial structure.

facing page: New display spaces and access routes within the building are constructed using present-day techniques and materials, with no blurring of the line between old and new.

CATHEDRAL MUSEUM LUCCA, ITALY

PIETRO CARLO PELLEGRINI ARCHITETTO, 1987–92

right: The Piazza Antelminelli prior to refurbishment.
facing page: Pellegrini's Cathedral Museum at Lucca looks to the Italian tradition
of introducing bold new interventions into historic complexes.

Lucca is one of the most satisfying and enjoyable cities in Italy. The historic core, now largely traffic-free, sits within the line of the tree-topped sixteenth-century ramparts and in one corner stands the Romanesque Duomo, foremost among the numerous churches of the city. The cathedral of San Martino enjoys a green setting to the east – partly the result of Fascist 'improvements' which removed a huddle of medieval buildings – and to the west faces on to the Piazza Antelminelli, a quiet square surrounded by *palazzi*, and set apart from the commercial life of the city. Its awe-inspiring interior contains many treasures, not least the ancient figure of Christ known as the *Volto Santo*. Like other great Italian churches, the cathedral possesses many portable treasures – vestments, plate, service books, manuscripts and pictures – while other items have been deposited from closed churches and monasteries in the city and diocese. After the closure of the cathedral museum some years ago, all these items were effectively put into store and were largely inaccessible to the public and to scholars, and there were concerns about the conservation of many of the objects.

Pellegrini's project to re-house the museum was made possible by a major donation from a regional bank, combined with support from the city and central government. The buildings next to the flank of the Duomo had been in ecclesiastical ownership for centuries and were latterly used to house the stored cathedral treasures. They included a group of storehouses, much altered over the centuries, facing on to an enclosed court, and a disused oratory of St Joseph, itself a dignified structure retaining many of its fittings. There was also the stump of a thirteenth-century tower, once attached to a patrician house on the site and which, to complicate things further, was an ancient cemetery. The complex was typical of Lucca, with its dense 'nougat' (as the critic Carla Bertolucci describes it) of buildings and spaces, public and private. The buildings were in a sound but dishevelled state and posed obvious problems for reuse: they consisted of a warren of small rooms, while the only access to upper floors was via a single narrow stone staircase. The conditions for conversion laid down by the *Comune* and the regional *Superintendenza* for historic buildings proscribed major structural alterations or any significant changes in the external appearance of the buildings.

Pellegrini's approach was informed by the precedents of Carlo Scarpa, BBPR and Franco Albini – bold and rigorous interventions in an entirely contemporary manner, serving modern needs and standing free of the ancient fabric without rhetoric or gimmicks. The project was grounded in thorough archaeological research into the site and the buildings. There had been many alterations and interventions over the centuries, so that a degree of restoration and simplification could equally restore lost spaces and provide the context for

a modern museum, with up-to-date standards of security, access and conservation. By keeping the new elements light and as transparent as possible, Pellegrini aimed to reveal the qualities of the old work as well as provide an agreeable modern environment for visitors. Accessing upper floors was a primary issue, addressed by the insertion of a new lightweight, freestanding steel stair, together with a lift, in an existing void. Choice of materials was another key issue in the project. New flooring in polished grey Matraia stone followed a local tradition, and was also in tune with the widespread use of steel for railings, stands for display cases and partitions on which paintings and other large objects are hung. The aim was to provide a contrast with the simply restored walls (bare brick or plain render) and timber ceilings. Display cases eschew deliberate austerity and are framed in fine woods, such as pear and cypress, on a steel base: they are both secure and beautiful.

Pellegrini's Lucca museum is a fine balance of restoration and radical intervention, the latter always clearly expressed – the new mezzanine floor, for example, stands back from the old brickwork and there are views to the ground floor of the building. The highest praise that can be given to any museum building is that it lets the exhibits dominate and at Lucca the copes, chalices, altarpieces and, not least, the precious adornments of the *Volto Santo* – used in the cathedral only once a year – are brilliantly displayed. The random, even circuitous, plan (a consequence of the conservative approach to the old fabric) adds to the sense of discovery and surprise, accentuated by the various horizontal and vertical views through the building.

A satisfying new architectural expression has emerged, despite the massive demands placed on the architect by the art conservators and the building conservationists. Externally, the transformation is, perhaps, under-expressed, so that many visitors remain unaware of the museum's existence, but this was a consequence of strict planning provisions. (Only the plain, metal-framed windows suggest that there is anything new and radical within.) The cathedral museums of Italy are one of the delights of the country – they are often charming survivals of an age when modern museological standards were unknown. But concerns about conservation and security make many of them an anomaly. Lucca has set a standard for others to follow. There is no longer the charming jumble of objects found in the past: everything is well-lit and properly labelled. But the approach of the architect has ensured that a sense of wonder, and, indeed, of the sacred, is retained. The Cathedral Museum is a microcosm of Lucca itself, a city with no great set-pieces, but a place where there are treasures to be discovered by anyone with the interest to seek them out.

above: The plan allows for views into the surrounding galleries.

facing page: Display techniques use modern technology to complement the artefacts – stands and cases are kept simple and unobtrusive.

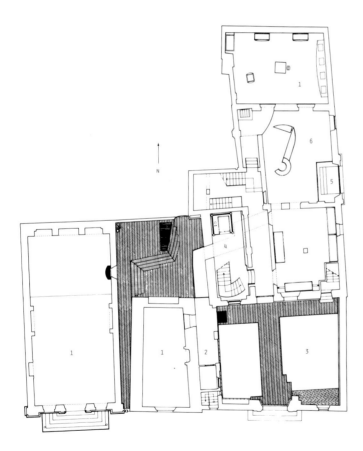

Ground-floor plan

1 Display space
2 Loggia
3 Courtyard garden

4 Lift
5 Entrance
6 Reception

facing page: The existing fabric has been repaired and cleaned and the old materials provide a pleasing contrast with new stone paving and steel stairs and rails.

ANDALUSIAN INSTITUTE OF HERITAGE SEVILLE, SPAIN
GUILLERMO VÁSQUEZ CONSUEGRA ARQUITECTO, 1991–95

The 1992 Seville Expo, celebrating the 500th anniversary of Columbus's discovery of America, reflected the ambitions of the southern Spanish region of Andalusia to emerge as a dynamic European region. The Expo produced an extraordinarily diverse display of new architecture from around the world, a striking contrast to the rich and dense historic fabric of the old city of Seville. Most of what was built for 1992 quickly disappeared after the end of the Expo, but there were more permanent benefits to the city. The Expo was sited on the island of La Cartuja in the Guadalquivir river, an area once occupied in part by a famous monastery (suppressed in the nineteenth century) and later an active seat of local industry. The buildings converted into a centre for the study and conservation of works of art by Guillermo Vásquez Consuegra incorporated substantial parts of the former monastery, which had been subsumed into a ceramics factory established by a British entrepreneur in 1839.

The core of the factory was the lay brothers' cloister, clearly apparent in the plan and in some exposed fragments of old work. Attached was a sprawl of later buildings, some of value, others no more than flimsy sheds. As is often the case, the architect's first task was to establish what was worth keeping. Vásquez Consuegra's instincts were archaeological in the best sense: to retain the evidence of the site's past, while recognizing that its more recent history had significance too. (The monumental bottle kilns obviously had to be retained.) There was to be no attempt to strip back the remains to the pre-industrial 'original'. In practical terms, the brief demanded a variety of spaces including restoration studios and laboratories (the Institute is part of a campaign to conserve thousands of works of art in churches and local museums in the region), a specialist library and extensive archive, lecture rooms and galleries open to the public. (As well as carrying out conservation work, the Institute aims to train conservators for the future.) The programme involved both some demolition and the construction of new buildings on part of the site. Refurbishment was guided by a concern to protect old fabric, but to add to it in an entirely contemporary way. Where the old buildings could not meet modern needs, new structures were added – the restoration workshops, for example, with a lofty roof structure designed to maximize north light, are entirely new but clearly within a tradition of industrial architecture. There were good practical reasons for keeping much of the existing complex, coupled with a need to achieve a workable plan.

The exhibition and administration block showcase the architect's approach to the older buildings, treating them as 'a stimulating body of material for the new project'. The bones of the building, its galleried basilican interior, is stripped of accretions and simply toplit. The offices on the first floor are modern insertions, which stand free of the old structure (originally a granary or storehouse for the monastery). Vásquez Consuegra uses modern materials – including fair-faced concrete and steel – with conviction and panache. A relic of nineteenth-century industry has been transformed to accommodate the highly specialized needs of twentieth-century museology.

194

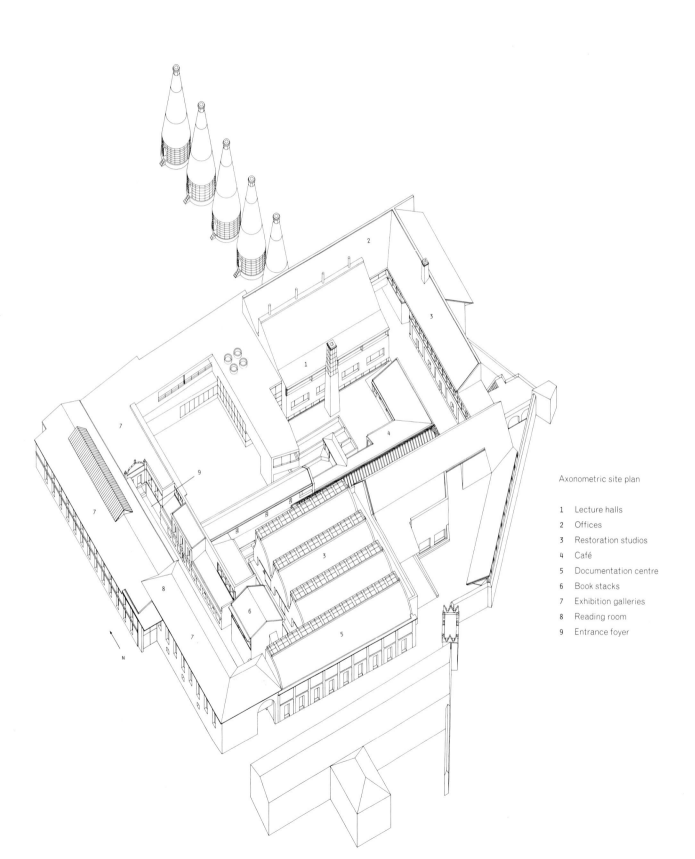

Axonometric site plan

1 Lecture halls
2 Offices
3 Restoration studios
4 Café
5 Documentation centre
6 Book stacks
7 Exhibition galleries
8 Reading room
9 Entrance foyer

left: The new insertions are simply and crisply detailed.

right: One of the exhibition galleries.

left and right: The dramatically top-lit restoration studios.

following page: Vásquez Consuegra's transformation is structured around the most interesting remnants of the site's rich history – such as the monumental bottle kilns.

MUSEUM OF FINE ARTS LILLE, FRANCE

JEAN-MARC IBOS AND MYRTO VITART, 1990–97

The Museum of Fine Arts in Lille is generally considered to be the leading art museum in France outside Paris, with holdings that range across the whole history of European art, including a particularly striking collection of works by Van Dyck and Rubens. The acquisitions of the great northern French city were brought together at the end of the nineteenth century in a vast and imposing new building by Berard and Delmas (1892–95) which forms one side of the Place de la République and is a fine but over-detailed example of the neo-Renaissance manner of the period.

The existing museum attracted relatively few visitors and was critically slated for its poor displays and standards of conservation: the commission to refurbish and extend it was part of the wave of activity in Lille that followed the opening of the new London–Lille–Brussels Eurostar rail service. (The Euralille project, masterplanned by Rem Koolhaas, is equally a product of the mood of regeneration. Bernard Tschumi's Le Fresnoy scheme (pages 134–141) is a further spin-off.)

Grand as Berard and Delmas's building is, it was never constructed as intended: a further U-shaped wing, completing the enclosure of a central courtyard, was planned but never built. During the 1930s the museum was extended by glazing over the central court to create an enclosed atrium, with a new staircase to serve the upper floors, while a new wing of offices was built in the 1970s along the southern edge of the building. By totally closing off the museum on this side, the authorities apparently accepted that the ambitions of the past were finally written off.

Ibos and Vitart's ambitious and costly (FF250 million) reconstruction project was won in an invited competition in 1990, and combined – typically for the museum projects of the late twentieth century – faithful restoration and radical new interventions. A spur to the project was provided by the controversial decision to relocate 16 of the famous large-scale town models, formerly shown at the Invalides in Paris, to Lille. This prompted a reconsideration of the whole display policy embracing paintings, sculpture, ceramics and medieval antiquities. The competition brief also asked for a strategy for the public and administrative spaces of the museum, providing up-to-the-minute amenities for staff and visitors.

The restoration element of Ibos and Vitart's scheme included the demolition of the 1970s offices and the staircase that half-filled the atrium; restoration of all galleries, with new lighting and furnishings; and the refurbishment of brick-vaulted basements to house the medieval and Renaissance galleries. There were bold (and even contentious) touches: vast hanging light fittings by Gaetano Pesce – 'two bags containing objects in fragments, witnesses of everyday reality' – in the entrance hall and more lighting sunk into the finely formed nineteenth-century masonry vaults. A café and bookshop were formed in the arcades of the atrium.

On the whole, however, the work inside the nineteenth-century building is not controversial or surprising, though the transformation is sufficiently dramatic for anyone who knew the museum before 1990. What happens beyond it is extraordinary and highly memorable. Ibos and Vitart's competition entry spoke of 'opening up' the museum to the city. Where there was once a barrier of offices on the southern elevation of the old building, there is now a glazed arcade to a new open, public court. Below this space is the new 700 square-metre (7,534 square-foot) top-lit temporary exhibitions gallery, which connects at basement level to the new glazed 'blade' building, containing a restaurant at ground level and administrative offices above. The strikingly slim 'blade' is both a much-needed termination of the court and an ethereal semi-presence, all glass and reflecting the decorated bulk of Berard and Delmas's building. It is double-glazed externally, in clear glass, within in-figured glazing in abstract red and gold patterning. The façade, the particular responsibility of project architect Sophie N'Guyen, working with Y. R. M. Anthony Hunt Associates, is a true work of art in its own right, an art object for the city. Indeed, the new extension is the most striking recent building in the centre of Lille. It makes no demands on its venerable nineteenth-century neighbour and gives no deference to it. Ibos and Vitart have given the city a new landmark and have infused life into an institution which seemed half-moribund.

above: The basement level of the existing building has been reconstructed to give access to a new underground gallery.
right: The atrium, originally the central court which was glazed over in the 1930s, has been freed of the staircase that largely filled it and made into a new focus, with a bookshop and café.

Ground-floor plan showing the relationship between the existing building and Ibos and Vitart's new 'blade', containing a restaurant and museum administration, which is linked to the old building at basement level.

1 Sculpture and ceramics galleries
2 Atrium
3 Entrance
4 External courtyard
5 Café

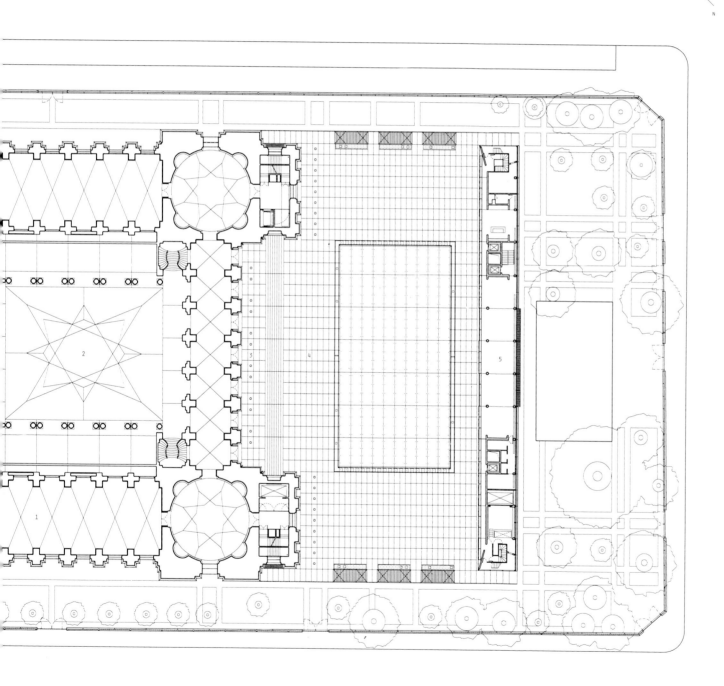

N

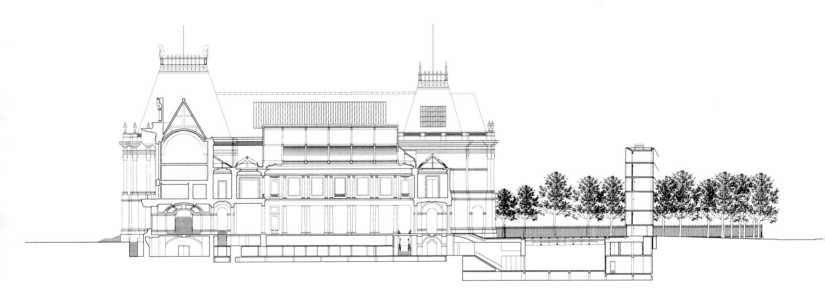

The relationship between old and new is clear in the longitudinal section.

above: Externally, the 'blade' is translucent and semi-reflective, an elusive yet memorable
presence, complementing rather than challenging the nineteenth-century façades.
right: Inside, the glazing provides a benign, naturally lit interior for museum staff.

COLEGIO NACIONAL MEXICO CITY, MEXICO

TEODORO GONZÁLEZ DE LEÓN ARQUITECTO, 1993–94

The convent and college of La Enseñanza is one of the great institutions of the ancient centre of Mexico City, among the world's largest historic urban cores. The late eighteenth-century monastic and school complex has, however, changed its function many times over the last two centuries. Parts of it have served as prison, law court, school for the blind and student hostel. In the 1940s the whole complex, apart from the church, was colonized by the education ministry, the legal archives of the state and the prestigious, newly-formed National College. In the late 1980s the decision was taken to expand the college into the space (around 7,400 square metres/79,653 square feet) formerly occupied by other public bodies. Finance was provided in 1992 and conversion work began the following year.

The old buildings had been extensively altered 50 years previously, with the historic fabric randomly mutilated and masked by additions. Original roofs, for instance, had been replaced by flat concrete slabs. The buildings focus on three open cloisters, one of which had been the base of the National College from the 1940s. These cloisters remained basically unchanged. The brief for the expansion scheme provided for a new library, lecture halls, offices, refectory and a main hall, suitable for conferences and other large gatherings. Radical internal changes were needed. In the east wing, a library extends over three floors. The new main hall is a full-height space, carved out of another wing. Introducing natural light into the reused buildings was a key issue and was achieved by cutting openings into the roofs. The use of glass-block floors allowed daylight to enter the lower levels of the buildings. Previously gloomy spaces have become open and luminous. The aesthetic of the transformation scheme mixes traditional stucco with exposed concrete and wood. New elements, such as lifts exposed in glass, are designed in an entirely modern fashion, with no attempt to disguise their contemporaneity.

This project is seen as a marker for the repair and reuse of the thousands of Mexico City's historic buildings, some semi-derelict, others under-used. The strengthening of higher education as an activity in the historic core is seen as an augury for further regeneration.

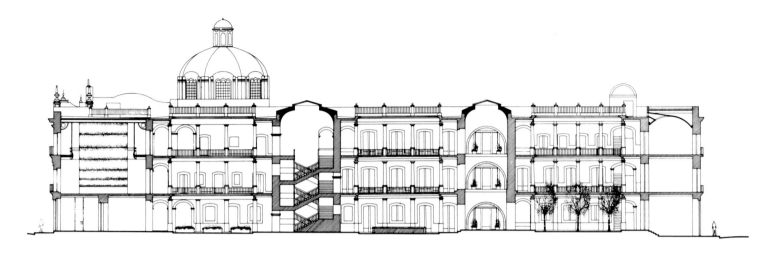

Section

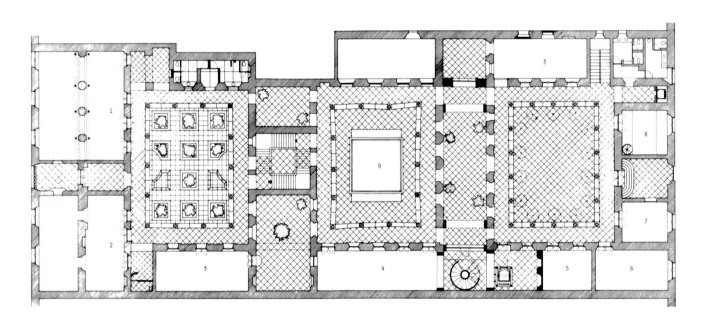

Ground-floor plan

N ——→

1 Cafeteria
2 Bookshop
3 Lecture hall
4 Library
5 Library reception

6 Administration
7 Storeroom
8 Basement archive
9 Fountain

left: The main auditorium.

right: Previously gloomy spaces have become open and luminous.

MUSEUM OF CONTEMPORARY ART BERLIN, GERMANY

JOSEF-PAUL KLEIHUES, 1989–96

In some countries, such as the USA and Britain, redundant railway buildings have posed problems of reuse, which are usually exacerbated by their grand scale. In Germany, the railway heritage was decimated by wartime bombing. Berlin suffered badly. (One of the major casualties, the splendid Anhalter Bahnhof, was left as a gutted shell and was torn down by the DDR in the 1960s.) The original Hamburger Bahnhof, the terminus for trains from Hamburg, was built in 1845–47, the iron and glass sheds being prefaced by a handsome neoclassical frontage in stone by Ferdinand Wilhelm Holz. (The plan of the station was unusual, in that tracks ran through arches in the terminal building to turntables, used to turn around locomotives.) The building was a key monument of the first German railway age, but after less than 40 years of use it was closed and trains were diverted to a new station. In 1904–6 the building was converted to a museum of transport and engineering, a use which continued until the Second World War, when it was damaged but not destroyed. The museum conversion, designed by Ernst Schwartz, included the construction in 1912–15 of gallery wings flanking the main frontage, which were in keeping with the original building.

The Hamburger Bahnhof survived in a semi-moribund cocoon, with many of its exhibits still extant but with no public access, from 1945 until 1984, when it passed into the hands of the West German authorities. A well-attended series of trial exhibitions led to a decision to convert it into a modern art museum. A 1989 competition was won by Kleihues. While the transformation of the building was underway, the Wall came down and the project took its place as part of the renaissance of the new capital of a united Germany. (Just across the Invalidenstrasse, the Lehrter Bahnhof – another wartime loss – is being rebuilt by von Gerkan, Marg as a key element in Berlin's public transport strategy.) Kleihues sought to retain the historic identity of the station/transport museum, while radically transfiguring its image. Railways were the symbol of change in nineteenth-century Germany. Now, contemporary art has a similar role in challenging established patterns of life and thought.

Kleihues much admired the existing buildings for their rational elegance, part of a tradition which linked Schinkel and von Klenze, via Behrens, to Mies and the Modern Movement. The train shed (later main exhibition hall) had been flanked by two solid wings which Kleihues replaced with new gallery blocks. These galleries are top-lit and barrel-vaulted in deference to the tradition of railway architecture. Externally they are clad in thin aluminium (or glass) panels contained within a steel-framed, strongly expressed structural system, of great steel buttresses sitting on a limestone base and topped by a stone parapet. (Perhaps there are memories here of Behrens's famous turbine factory.) Service zones separate the new galleries from the main hall, which has been cleaned, repainted and refloored but not otherwise altered. The architect's intention was to echo the geometry of the original structure: the section of the new galleries is the classic Vitruvian circle within a square. Kleihues's own sublime geometry is concerned with the dialogue, central to all his work, between the classical tradition and modernity.

Interventions to the nineteenth-century buildings were kept to a minimum and detailed with fastidious care. The extreme minimalism of the new fit-out – granite paving, white-painted steel stairs and rails and white plaster walls – provides a neutral context not only for paintings but for large-scale installation art. Kleihues has been an active and sometimes acerbic commentator on the reconstruction of Berlin. His reassemblage of Berlin's 'lost' railway terminus has produced not only an excellent container for contemporary art, but an exemplar of the way that uncompromising modern design can enhance an old building.

213

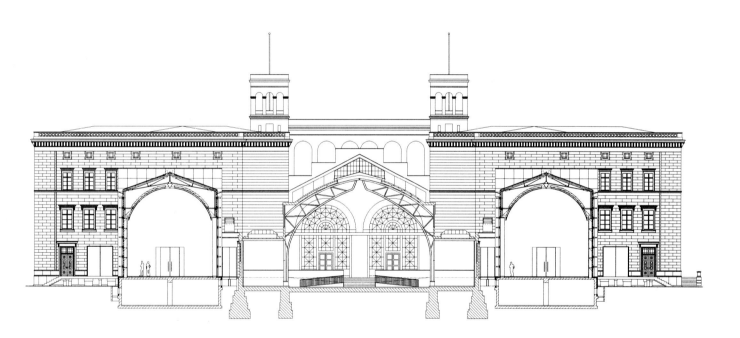

above: Section through the transformed building: new galleries – only one has been built so far – flank the refurbished train shed.

facing page: The bridge over the entrance doors connects the two new staircases.

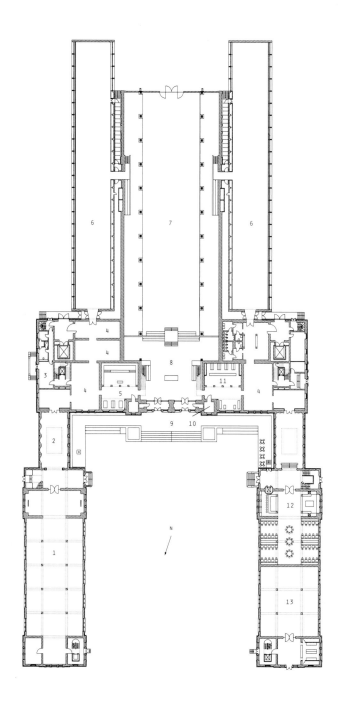

Ground-floor plan

1   Joseph Beuys gallery   8   Entrance hall
2   Lobby   9   Terrace
3   Staff entrance   10 Porch
4   Exhibition space   11 Cloakroom
5   Bookshop   12 Restaurant
6   Large gallery   13 Function gallery
7   Historical hall

The nineteenth-century train shed has a rare elegance that has been respected in the transformation project and which well complements the display of large art works.

above: The barrel vault in the new gallery admits both artificial light and controlled daylight.

facing page: The first of the flanking galleries to be built provides a contrast in materials and form to the existing fabric.

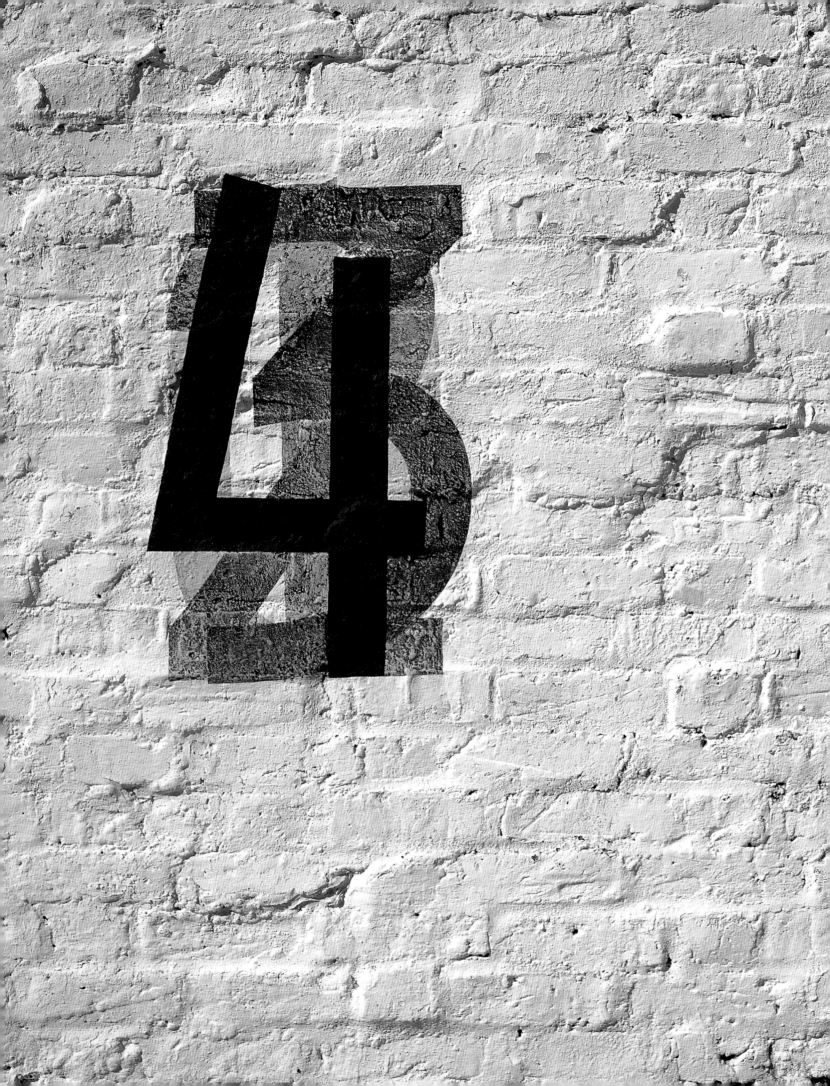

CHAPTER 4
THE FUTURE

The process of transformation is open-ended, limited only by the endurance of the components that make up a building. The use of a building may change many times during its lifetime, but transformation does not necessarily imply a change of use. The idea of a museum, a parliament house or even a railway station is different today from that which prevailed even a few decades ago. Norman Foster's reconstruction of the British Museum provides an enlarged and improved space for education, lectures, drinking coffee, buying books and souvenirs and even merely sitting down and watching other visitors. All are part of the museum 'experience' of the late twentieth century. (The director of the Museum of Modern Art, New York, foresees the future of MOMA as 'a loud, cacophonous environment in which fun is had by all'.') Beyond the razzmatazz, however, Foster's scheme has architectural integrity, not least in restoring a great central court lost to public view for well over a century.

Foster's other great transformational project due for completion at the close of the twentieth century, the Berlin Reichstag, also reinforces the historic use of a building. Yet the Reichstag has been a sad shell since its burning on the eve of the Second World War, its interior banally reconstructed during the 1950s. The scheme eschews restoration, external or internal, in favour of a new grandeur which is entirely of today and entirely democratic. The building is purged of memories of Kaiserism, Nazism and of a divided Germany and reborn as a symbol of unity – and of the renaissance of Berlin as possibly the key city in the new Europe. The restoration of New York's Grand Central Terminal is equally symbolic. In a particularly American way, the project combines public and commercial objectives and draws on funding from public and private sectors. There is a price to be paid: intensive retail and restaurant uses. Yet the balance is held and a symbol of civic pride reborn.

In Western countries, the future of architecture appears to lie largely in transforming existing buildings. Often, that process will be matter of fact, a proper use of resources. Underlying it is the imperative to reduce energy consumption and protect supplies – compact cities make sense. Occasionally, there will be opportunities for landmark schemes which can bolster not just the physical fabric, but also the spirit, of a city. The value of the past is being understood, not just in London and Paris but also in Tokyo and Shanghai. As Far Eastern economies mature, the true value of buildings and whole cities will be appreciated. The potential for combining old fabric and new ideas to create a resource for the future is almost limitless.

1. V. Newhouse, *Towards a New Museum*, New York 1998, p. 191

TATE GALLERY OF MODERN ART BANKSIDE, LONDON, UK

HERZOG & DE MEURON ARCHITEKTEN, 1994–2000

facing page: Herzog & de Meuron's competition-winning scheme for the new Tate Gallery of Modern Art proposed few changes to the exterior of the old power station, except for the addition of a top floor 'light beam'.
left: The interior showing the converted turbine hall, the main public space within the building.

Zurich-based Herzog & de Meuron's victory in the two-stage competition (1994–95) for a new Tate Gallery, 'the MOMA of London', housed in the former Bankside power station, pleased conservationists who thought the building (completed 1963, with architectural cladding by Sir Giles Gilbert Scott) worthy of retention. While other competitors (notably runner-up David Chipperfield) proposed radical alterations to the building, Herzog & de Meuron's scheme left it externally largely intact. On the other hand, some critics felt that the building imposed a strong – and not necessarily positive – image of the past on an institution devoted to the present and the future.

Bankside, just across the Thames from St Paul's, was controversial when first built, but it provided a highly practical container for the new Tate, a key millennium project funded by the National Lottery, and expected to attract two million visitors annually. The vast interior included a huge turbine hall, 152 metres (500 feet) long and 26 metres (85 feet) high, and scope for providing 11,150 square metres (120,000 square feet) of gallery space – larger than the total area of the existing Tate Gallery, Millbank. The transformation project, ranking in scale alongside Paris's Parc de la Villette and Turin's Lingotto, aims to retain the best qualities of the old building while infusing it with elements that are entirely new and innovative. The project is seen to be as much about regeneration as it is about reuse in that it will transform the long-neglected South Bank (see pages 124–127). The Bankside Tate will be linked to the City by a new bridge, designed by Sir Norman Foster and Sir Anthony Caro.

The focus of the building will be the converted turbine hall, stripped of machinery and turned into a huge public galleria. The hall will be approached by a great ramp from the west, with additional entrances from the river terrace and bridge. Galleries and other spaces extend along the river frontage of the building.

The retention of the 99 metre- (325 foot-) high chimney was a key feature of Herzog & de Meuron's winning scheme, ensuring that the structure will remain a landmark, though detached from the bulk of the building by the excision of the 'shoulders' that flanked it. Bankside's new image will be based on the contrast between the solid vertical emphasis of the chimney and the more ethereal, semi-transparent 'light beam' extending across the façade and providing restaurants and other public rooms with fine river views. Although a massive sub-station will be retained on site for the foreseeable future, the long-term expectation is for the Tate to occupy the entire building, which will result in, potentially, the largest modern art museum in the world.

The Bankside project loses none of its inspirational quality from being pragmatic and accretive in its approach. The completed scheme will certainly reflect the architects' fastidious approach to detailing and their consummate mastery of the use of natural light. The bravura of the conversion scheme is due, in part at least, to the lack of planning constraints – Bankside is not a listed building. The scheme retains the strength of the old industrial structure (Scott's contribution was essentially cosmetic) though inflected with the tough elegance of forward-looking architecture, gratifyingly free of the urge to make statements or impose its own rhetoric on the past. Bankside establishes a new standard for architectural transformation.

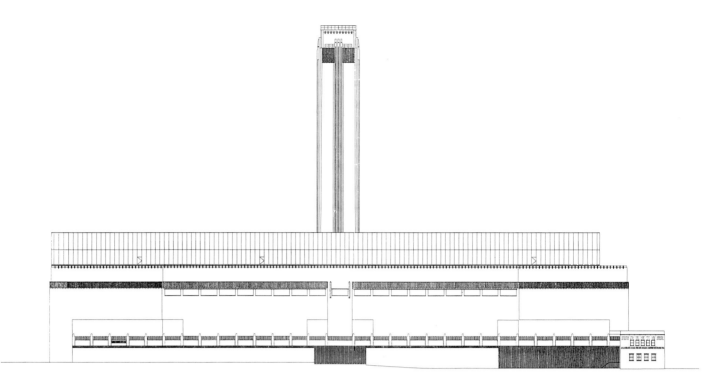

Elevation

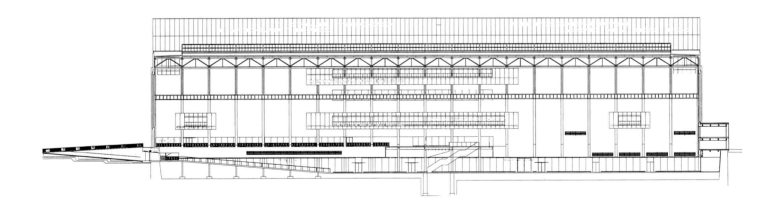

Cross-section. Levels 3, 4 and 5 contain the main exhibition spaces. A restaurant and members'
room are situated on levels 6 and 7. The turbine hall acts like a street, a central focus point for
the different gallery spaces.

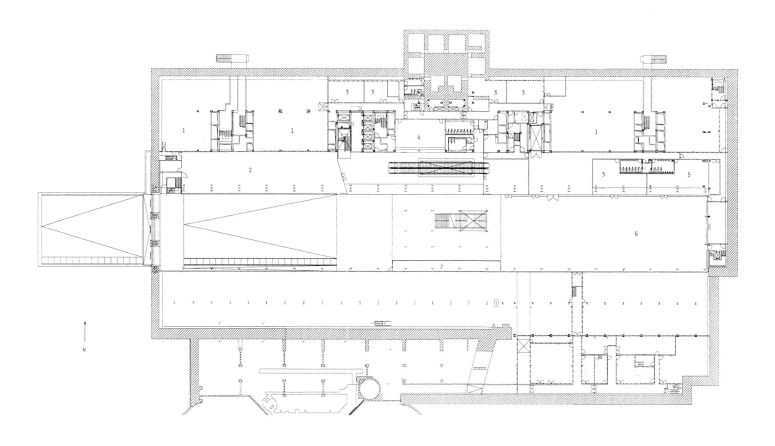

Level 1

1   Plant
2   Shop
3   Storeroom
4   Locker room

5   Workshop
6   Turbine hall
7   Tickets and information

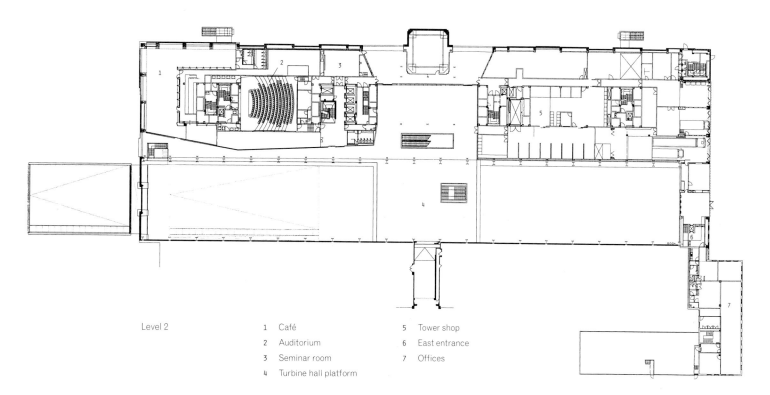

Level 2

1   Café
2   Auditorium
3   Seminar room
4   Turbine hall platform

5   Tower shop
6   East entrance
7   Offices

GRAND CENTRAL TERMINAL DEVELOPMENT NEW YORK CITY, USA

BEYER BLINDER BELLE, ARCHITECTS AND PLANNERS, 1990–98

facing page: Section through the terminal as transformed: cafés and restaurants occupy the galleries around the main concourse. The lower-level (suburban) concourse houses a food court and shops.

Grand Central Terminal was always much more than a railway station. Replacing an earlier station on the site, it opened in 1913 and was the catalyst for – and the centrepiece of – a massive remodelling of mid-town Manhattan, masterminded by engineer William Wilgus and involving hugely profitable 'air rights' development above the rail tracks and the creation, in effect, of a new city district. Designed by architects Warren & Wetmore, the station itself was intended to dominate and to impress.

Whereas the first Grand Central had focused on the arched train shed, its successor buried the (electrically powered) trains out of sight. The heart of the station was the grandiose upper-level concourse, referred to as 'the finest big room in New York', serving long-distance traffic, including the crack 20th Century Limited service to Chicago. Suburban services were served by a more modest but still elegant lower concourse.

The decline of Grand Central began in the 1950s, as long-distance rail travel withered under competition from the airlines. A series of schemes involving the demolition of all or part of the station led to a campaign to save the building, which came to be seen as being all the more precious to New York after the lamentable destruction of Pennsylvania Station in 1963. After prolonged planning and legal battles (which lasted a quarter of a century and ended in a Supreme Court victory for conservationists in 1978) Grand Central's future seemed assured. Indeed, it was heavily used by 30,000 rail commuters daily and by many more people for whom it was an interchange and a meeting place. But the shabby condition of the building in the 1980s reflected years of indecision and lack of investment. Its plight was symbolized for many by the vast illuminated Kodak advertisement that filled one wall of the main concourse. Grand Central had become a billboard. With all long-distance train services re-routed into the rebuilt Penn Station, Grand Central became the responsibility of the Metropolitan Transportation Authority and Metro North Railroad.

In 1990, the Kodak sign was taken down and plans to totally refurbish the station were announced, with Beyer Blinder Belle (BBB) as architects. The masterplan addressed the multiple function of Grand Central as transport hub, commercial centre and civic monument. The restoration in 1991–92 of the main waiting room demonstrated the potential of the project. In 1996 work began on refurbishing the remainder of the complex, a $200 million operation funded by a mix of public and private capital. The key issue was to balance the various roles of the building. The 1980s restoration of Union Station, Washington DC, where passengers were far more sparse, had turned a public building into a shopping mall, with the original function of the station all but forgotten. BBB's masterplan aimed to make the station work better for commuters by generating revenue from commercial development. But the latter was kept within bounds and not allowed to dominate.

The main concourse is the centrepiece, as ever. Under the completely renovated ceiling, painted with a representation of the night sky, the concourse has been given a much extended use, with restaurants and cafés along the three sides of the first-floor gallery. Previously, gallery level was accessible only by the grand west staircase leading to Vanderbilt Avenue. BBB duplicated this staircase in replica on the east side of the concourse, reviving an unexecuted plan by Warren & Wetmore. The ramps leading to the lower concourse, long sunk below inserted floors of offices, were now removed to allow daylight to penetrate the lower level. The suburban concourse itself has become a food court for informal eating, supplementing the historic Oyster Bar. (Escalators, unobtrusively slotted in, provide additional access for train users.) New retail outlets have been concentrated in a 'market' area between the upper concourse and the much improved entry from Lexington Avenue – nothing impedes the main concourse, which remains, in Philip Johnson's words 'the cathedral of New York'. The cleaning and reinstatement of features and materials throughout has visibly enhanced the building. The complete overhaul of services is less obvious but all the more vital.

Grand Central was once a test case in preservation law in the USA. Now it has become a monument to the powers of transformation. Although BBB's refurbishment has – at the insistence of city planners and Landmark Commission officials – adhered to the style of the original (even to the extent of dusting off 80-year-old plans), it has inaugurated a new era for the terminal, anchoring it more firmly than ever in the business and social life of the metropolis. The transformation of Grand Central reflects New York's pride in its past and faith in its future.

Grand Central remains a dominant monument in central Manhattan, despite the presence
of the MetLife (formerly Pan Am) building constructed on an adjacent site in the 1960s.

The great painted ceiling of the main concourse of Grand Central Terminal, showing the night stars, has been completely restored as part of the refurbishment programme.

THE AMERICAN CINEMATHEQUE AT THE EGYPTIAN THEATER LOS ANGELES, USA

HODGETTS + FUNG DESIGN ASSOCIATES, 1996–98

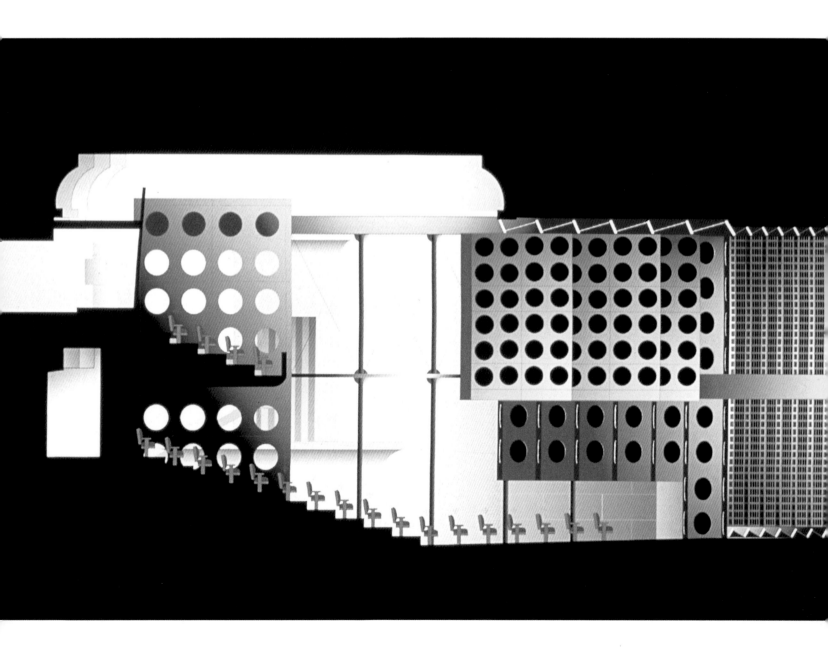

facing page: Hodgetts + Fung's refurbishment of the historic Egyptian Theater on Hollywood Boulevard provides a highly flexible new auditorium, with new sound and lighting technology supplied via moveable metal screens.
above: The refurbishment scheme embraces not just the theatre itself but the courtyard and the shopping area extending to the boulevard.

Grauman's Chinese Theater, opened in 1927, is one of the best-known tourist sights in Los Angeles. Its creator, Sid Grauman, was, however, also responsible for another exotic movie house, the 1922 Egyptian Theater on Hollywood Boulevard. Until its closure in 1992 following earthquake damage, the Egyptian Theater (designed by architects Meyer & Holler) was one of the curiosities of the city. Its heavily applied Egyptian styling – inspired by the unearthing of Tutankhamen's tomb – originally extended beyond the ornate frontage, facing on to a courtyard, to the interior, where the screen was framed by huge columns which might well have graced a pharaoh's mausoleum. (The internal decor was partly destroyed in an unfortunate 1960s rehabilitation – the proscenium arch was destroyed and the walls boarded over, hiding original details.)

Despite its landmark status, the building, derelict and vandalized, appeared to have no future until it was identified as the home of the American Cinematheque, a non-profit film theatre intended to screen both movie classics and the work of young directors as well as providing a showcase for the history of Hollywood. The initial steps towards rescuing the building were taken by the Los Angeles Community Redevelopment Agency – its rehabilitation was seen as an important element in the revival of Hollywood Boulevard. Architects Hodgetts + Fung faced a number of difficult decisions, the most pressing of which was to devise a method of saving the historic structure from total collapse. Next there was the issue of how far the lost details of the original might be restored and to what extent an entirely new design might play a part in the reconstruction – which was about transformation rather than restoration.

The use of the building was to change radically. The brief demanded a series of distinct spaces within the building, so that a verbatim reinstatement of the original 1,600-seat auditorium was out of the question. Instead, the new users required a highly flexible main theatre, seating between 400 and 700, and a smaller preview room, together with a much expanded lobby area. In the main space, audiences might see a silent classic, with Wurlitzer accompaniment, or the preview of a new film, requiring state-of-the-art sound equipment. The architects' strategy was to restore the historic fabric (built of hollow clay tile) externally and as an internal shell within which the new spaces can be seen as freestanding objects. In engineering terms, the existing structure had to be stabilized and reinforced. The new main theatre stands within the 1920s auditorium. (The space under the deep balcony, never very agreeable, has been reused for the smaller theatre and lobby.) New sound and lighting technology is catered for by means of moveable screens, which enclose the space and provide fixings for lights, speakers and ductwork. Perforations in the screens allow glimpses of the restored 1920s decor with acoustic screens sliding across the openings when a film is being shown. The 45 metre- (150 foot-) long forecourt, opening off the boulevard, was a key feature of the Egyptian Theatre as originally conceived. It was a lively place, lined with shops and an external foyer where audiences gathered before performances. Over the years, it became badly compromised and largely concealed by a marquee structure. Hodgetts + Fung are reinstating the open space with shops and cafés topped by a new roof garden as an amenity both for audiences and for the public. The original entrance portico is being faithfully restored.

Los Angeles has a rather mixed record of caring for its past. Tourists flock there to seek out the history of the film industry, but there is all too little for them to see. The American Cinematheque does something to remedy this omission while ensuring the future of a well-loved local landmark. The scheme has preserved the past, but without sentimentality and with an infusion of the new spirit of Los Angeles architecture.

THE REICHSTAG BERLIN, GERMANY

FOSTER AND PARTNERS, 1992–1999

facing page: Foster's restoration of the former Reichstag as the parliament
house of the new Germany reinstates the building as a focus of the capital and
the seat of the Bundestag.

right: The roof structure deflects controlled daylight into the chamber below,
as well as providing support for an elevated viewing deck.

The reconstruction of the Reichstag forms the symbolic focus of Berlin's emergence as the capital of a reunited Germany. Foster and Partners were chosen as architects for the scheme after an invited competition, a victory that reflected the practice's strong track record in Germany. The Reichstag building, a pompous monument of the late Imperial era, was badly damaged by fire in 1938 and further ravaged in the Second World War, when it was shelled by the Red Army. It was rather perfunctorily reconstructed in the 1950s.

The rebuilding project was inevitably controversial, given the Reichstag's position in twentieth-century German history. Foster's first proposal was radically transformational, placing the old parliament house on a new podium topped by a public square. The whole complex was to be covered by a lightweight and symbolic roof 'umbrella' – thus recasting the problematic image of the Reichstag – and also assisting energy conservation by deflecting light into the building and assisting a natural ventilation strategy. The decision to abandon this radical scheme produced revised proposals, more modest in intent and in cost, though the commitment to low-energy technology remained. There was no attempt to restore the original plan of the building, although the original ceremonial entrance, long blocked, has been reopened – it is now accessible to all, since public access to the nation's democratic forum is a basic ingredient of the scheme. The spectacular parliamentary chamber forms the heart of the building and is topped by a glazed oculus. Above rises a dome, not a restoration of that which burned in 1938 but certainly incorporating memories of the past. (A number of possible variants were discussed before the final form was agreed.) A great scoop within the dome structure is key to the natural ventilation system: the dome also contains batteries of energy-generating photo-voltaic cells. Finally, the dome incorporates a gently sloped ramp providing public access to a viewing gallery on the summit. Far from being a cosmetic make-over of a worrying relic, the Reichstag project attempts to come to terms with history – the marks of shells and bullets and graffiti left by Russian soldiers are being preserved in places to remind Germans of the Second World War and the Cold War. Elsewhere careful restoration of the nineteenth-century fabric contrasts with new interventions reflecting the general philosophy of the scheme, which is boldly transformationist. In line with this, the reconstructed building will open in 1999 as the symbol of a new nation.

The dome under construction. The helical ramp will provide access to a viewing deck.

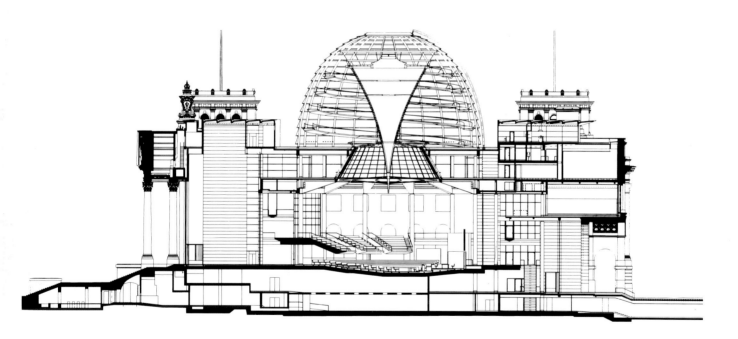

At the heart of the building lies the circular plenary chamber where the parliament
will sit. The glazed structure deflects daylight into the plenary chamber below, and
is an integral part of the natural ventilation system.

OBERBAUM CITY BERLIN, GERMANY

ARCHITEKTEN REICHEL & STAUTH, ARCHITEKTEN SCHWEGER & PARTNER, WEP EFFINGER PARTNERS, MARCO GOETZ KATR
HOOTZ ARCHITEKTEN, ARCHITEKTEN HUXOLL & SCHWAB, ARCHITECT T.V.D. VALENTYN AND REGINA SCHUH, 1993–2000

The vast complex of redundant industrial buildings – with a total area of 46,000 square metres (495,139 square feet) – that is being transformed into Oberbaum City was formerly the Osram light bulb factory, constructed in phases between 1906 and 1914. By the 1920s, over 6,000 people were employed there. The Osram operation was extinguished after 1945, but light bulb production continued under the East German regime – only to be closed down as uneconomic following German reunification.

The Oberbaum City project reflects the rediscovery of rundown and hitherto inaccessible quarters of Berlin which has followed the removal of the Wall. Its mix of commercial and residential use is in a well-established Berlin tradition, represented, for example, by the 1900s Hackesche Höfe development (recently refurbished, see pages 42–49) – and is intended as an important element in the regeneration of the eastern half of the city. (Up to 6,000 new jobs are envisaged within the scheme.) The site is close to the river Spree and the recently-restored Oberbaum Bridge, which carries a U-bahn line into the heart of the new development. The former factory buildings, as elegant as they were stoutly constructed, provided obvious potential for reuse, while there was also scope for some new buildings. The first phase to be completed (in 1995) was entirely offices. Block 5, a particularly elegant structure of 1907 by Theodor Kampfmeyer, was converted in 1996–97 by architects Reichel & Stauth into offices, shops, restaurants and accommodation for the Berlin Design Centre. Attached to this block is a new building to be occupied by departments of the Technical University. The much larger Block 4, at the heart of the site, is being transformed by Reichel & Stauth as offices, with a small element of shops and restaurants. A new building alongside will contain 28,000 square metres (301,389 square feet) of residential space – 330 units in all. The new blocks have a rational, restrained aesthetic intended to mirror that of the existing buildings.

The overall approach towards transformation has been to eschew façadism. The 'bones' of the existing buildings have been retained as the basis for new internal layouts. (Heavy pollution of the factory blocks by mercury meant that, in any case, all existing cores had to be stripped out.) Some internal features have been retained.

Hamburg-based Schweger & Partner, a practice with a notable track record in the field of transformation, are reconstructing Block 3 (also by Kampfmeyer and the largest of the buildings) as the flagship of the entire scheme with a mix of offices and other uses. The building has been extended with a new glazed office tower sitting boldly on top of Kampfmeyer's brick façade. When lit up by night, the new tower will be a landmark across the city and a monument to the historic function of the site.

Schweger & Partner's transformation of Block 3 into the flagship for the entire project places a highly glazed tower on top of the massive 1900s block.

The existing buildings have a tough elegance which adapts well to new use.

THE BRITISH MUSEUM REDEVELOPMENT LONDON, UK

FOSTER AND PARTNERS, 1994-2001

facing page: Foster and Partners' 'Great Court' project for London's British Museum opens up the heart of the building – formerly occupied by the British Library – and provides a focus for millions of visitors.
above: The area around the former Reading Room, until recently occupied by book stacks, is the central circulation space of the transformed museum.
following page: The scheme covers the central court with a lightweight glazed roof. New visitor facilities will be arranged around the great drum of the new Reading Room.

Foster and Partners' £97 million millennium project for the British Museum in Bloomsbury was won in competition in summer 1994 and promises a heroic transformation of a great cultural institution comparable with I. M. Pei's reconstruction of the Louvre: the revamped museum is seen as an element in a new 'cultural route' across central London. The scheme builds on Foster's established record as a master of transformation, originating in more modest undertakings such as the Sackler Galleries within London's Royal Academy (completed in 1991).

The museum, one of London's greatest landmarks and tourist attractions and a prime monument of the Greek Revival, was constructed between the 1820s and 1850s to designs by Sir Robert Smirke. The famous circular Reading Room (made redundant by the opening in 1997 of the new British Library at St Pancras) was built in 1854–57, filling in a great open quadrangle. The Edward VII galleries to the north were an early twentieth-century addition by J. J. Burnet.

The Foster scheme focuses on the museum's heart, the Great Court, surrounding and encompassing the former Reading Room. Smirke had envisaged the 0.8 hectare (2 acre) open quadrangle as a busy public space, but it was little used and its loss was uncontroversial. In recent decades, however, visitor numbers have vastly increased – to 6 million annually – and the existing entrance hall is inadequate as a circulation space. There is also pressure for bigger and better shops, restaurants and such facilities as provided in big museums worldwide. The Reading Room itself was regarded as sacrosanct – the museum will maintain a library service there – but a new Great Court will be created around the Reading Room, where the immense book stacks of the British Library once stood. This huge and dramatic space will be covered by a lightweight glazed roof and will form the natural destination of visitors entering via Smirke's

great portico. (The much altered original Smirke façades, unseen for nearly 150 years, will be carefully restored and the now lost southern portico will be rebuilt.) The drum-shaped Reading Room will become a largely freestanding object, encircled by processional staircases leading to the first-floor galleries. The forecourt to the museum, cleared of parking and re-landscaped, will provide an external preface to the internal public space – both areas will be open for extended hours, even when galleries are closed.

An important factor in the redevelopment of the British Museum is the reuniting of its collections: from 1970 to 1997 lack of space obliged the Museum to outhouse its Ethnography Department. The Foster scheme will restore the outstanding ethnographical collections to Bloomsbury, housing them in new galleries below the Great Court, along with a new lecture theatre and other educational facilities. Upper-level mezzanines in the Great Court, elliptical in plan, will contain bookshops, restaurants and cafés. As in other Foster schemes, the dynamism of the idea is likely to be matched by a close concern for detail and technical performance. The huge roof of the Great Court, for example, is designed to provide controlled daylight without glare, while eliminating solar gain. It will cover a serene space at the heart of not only the museum, but of London, and will be one of the great public forums of the twenty-first century.

243

PROJECT CREDITS

AGRONOMIC FACULTY, GEMBLOUX
1,830 square metres/19,660 square feet
Architect/Interior Design: Samyn and Partners, Architects and Engineers
Client: Facultés des Sciences Agronomiques de Gembloux
Project Team: Philippe Samyn, G. Andre, Y. Avoiron, A. Charon, K. de Mulder, F. El Sayed, L. Finet, D. Melotte, N. Milo, M. Patel, R. Tapia, P. Vleurick
Main Contractor: Thiran-Bajart
Structural Engineer: Samyn and Partners Sprl and Setesco s.a.
Mechanical Engineers: Samyn and Partners; FTI s.a.

THE AMERICAN CINEMATHEQUE AT THE EGYPTIAN THEATER, LOS ANGELES
2,550 square metres/27,450 square feet
Architect/Interior Design: Hodgetts + Fung Design Associates
Client: American Cinematheque
Project Team: Craig Hodgetts, Hsin-Ming Fung, Eric Holmquist
Main Contractor: Turner Construction Company
Historic Conservation Consultants: Historic Resources Group
Structural Engineer: Englekirk & Sabol, Inc.
Mechanical Engineer: ACCO (air conditioning)

ANDALUSIAN INSTITUTE OF HERITAGE, SEVILLE
13,248 square metres/142,600 square feet
Architect/Interior Design: Guillermo Vásquez Consuegra Arquiteco
Client: Consejeria de Cultura y Medio Ambiente Junta de Andalucia
Project Team: Joaquin Amaya, Andres Lopez, Jorge Vásquez Consuegra
Main Contractor: Construcciones Diego Cabeza
Historical Conservation Consultants: Archaeology Services (Junta de Andalucia)
Structural Engineer: Juan Rueda
Mechanical Engineer: Master s.a.
Quantity Surveyor: Marcos Vásquez Consuegrá

MARIO BELLINI STUDIO, MILAN
1,600 square metres/17,220 square feet
Architect and Interior Design: Mario Bellini Associati s.r.l.
Client: Mario Bellini Associati
Project Team: G. Bonfanti, E. Bruschi, C. Malnati
Main Contractor: COGED, Cologno al Serio
Structural Engineer: R. Ercoli
Quantity Surveyor: Mario Bellini Associati

BILLINGSGATE MARKET CONVERSION, LONDON
11,200 square metres/120,550 square feet
Architect: Richard Rogers Partnership
Client: Citicorp/Citibank

Project Team: Richard Rogers, Mike Davies, John Young, Marco Goldschmied, Laurie Abbott, Graham Stirk, Andrew Morris, Avtar Lotay, John Lowe, Malcolm McGowen, Amanda Levette, Pierre Botchi
Main Contractor: Taylor Woodrow Management Contracting Ltd
Structural Engineer: Ove Arup & Partners
Mechanical Engineer: Ove Arup & Partners (services)
Quantity Surveyor: Hanscombe Partnership

BRITISH COUNCIL OFFICES, PRAGUE
1,500 square metres/16,140 square feet
Architect/Interior Design: Jestico & Whiles
Client: The British Council
Collaborating Architect: Surpmo Atelier (structural engineer)
Main Contractor: Pirea/Stamont
Quantity Surveyor: Jiri Pomeje, Prague

BRITISH MUSEUM REDEVELOPMENT, LONDON
6,030 square metres/64,900 square feet
Architect: Foster and Partners
Client: The British Museum
Project Team: Sir Norman Foster, Spencer de Grey, Giles Robinson
Main Contractor: Mace
Historical Conservation Consultant: Giles Quarme
Structural Engineer/Mechancial Engineer: Buro Happold
Quantity Surveyor: Northcroft

CATHEDRAL MUSEUM, LUCCA
1,500 square metres/16,150 square feet
Architect/Interior Design: Pietro Carlo Pellegrini Architetto
Client: Arcidiocesi di Lucca
Main Contractors: Graziano Nottoli; Nardini & Turchi
Historical Conservation Consultant: Clara Baracchini, Maria Teresa Filieri, Superintendents of the 'Beni Architettonici Ambientali, Artistici e Storici di Pisa'
Structural Engineer: Ingegnere Giovanni Ciancaglini

CENTRE FOR ART AND MEDIA TECHNOLOGY, KARLSRUHE
70,900 square metres/763,210 square feet
Architect: Architekten Schweger & Partner
Client: Stadt Karlsruhe, Kommunalbau Karlsruhe GmbH
Project Team: Prof. Peter Schweger, Hartmut H. Reifenstein, Bernhard Kohl, Wolfgang Schneider, Prof. Wilhelm Meyer
Main Contractors: Elmar Hellman (façade); Stahlbauwerk Müller GmbH (steelwork)
Structural Engineer: Janssen & Stocklin Ingenieurbüro; Sobek Ingenieurbüro im Bauwesen GmbH

THE CITADEL, LOS ANGELES
48,030 square metres/516,990 square feet
Architect: The Nadel Partnership
Design Architect: Sussman/Prejza & Company Inc.

Client: Trammell Crow Company; Copley Real Estate Advisors; City of Commerce Redevelopment Agency
Project Team: Deborah Sussman, Paul Prejza, O. Randolph Jones, Robert A. Jacques, Giorgio Lupu
Landscape Architect: Schwartz, Smith, Meyer (grand allée); Peridian Irvine (office buildings, factory outlet centre and hotel)
Main Contractors: HCB; CPW Inc. (restoration)
Historical Conservation Consultant: Martin Weil
Structural Engineer: Meyers, Nelson, Houghton
Mechanical Engineer: Hellman & Lober

CITIZENS' ART CENTRE, KANAZAWA
18,700 square metres/201,340 square feet
Architect: Ichiro Mizuno + Kanazawa Planning Research Company Ltd.
Client: City of Kanazawa
Main Contractors: Matsumoto Komuten Co. Ltd.; Saito Construction Co, Ltd.
Structural Engineer: Konishi Structural Engineers
Mechanical Engineer: Ogaki Consulting Engineers Office

COLEGIO NACIONAL, MEXICO CITY
7,400 square metres/79,650 square feet
Architect: Teodoro González de León Arquitecto
Client: El Colegio Nacional
Collaborating Architect: Miguel Barbachano Osorio
Interior Design: Luis A. De Regil
Main Contractor: Miguel Cornejo
Structural Engineer: Colinas de Buen

CULVER CITY, LOS ANGELES
Architect: Eric Owen Moss Architects

A.R. CITY
182,900 square metres/1,974,204 square feet
Client: Frederick Norton Smith
Project Team: Eric Owen Moss, Scott M. Nakao (project architect)

GARY GROUP BUILDING
4,500 square metres/48,440 square feet
Client: Frederick Norton Smith
Project Team: Eric Owen Moss, Jay Vanos (project architect)
Main Contractor: Jamik Inc.
Structural Engineer: Davis Design Group
Mechanical Engineer: AEC Systems

LINDBLADE TOWER
2,400 square metres/25,830 square feet
Client: Frederick Norton Smith
Project Team: Eric Owen Moss, Jay Vanos (project architect)
Main Contractor: Scott Gates Construction Company Inc.
Structural Engineer: The Office of Gordon Polon
Mechanical Engineer: AEC Systems

METAFOR
3,600 square metres/38,750 square feet
Client: Frederick and Laurie Samitaur Smith
Project Team: Eric Owen Moss, Jay Vanos (project architect)
Main Contractor: Samitaur Constructs
Structural Engineer: Kurily Szymanski Tchirkow
Mechanical Engineer: Fruchtman and Associates

8522 NATIONAL OFFICE BUILDING
16,500 square metres/177,600 square feet
Client: Frederick and Laurie Samitaur Smith
Project Team: Eric Owen Moss, Jay Vanos (project architect)
Main Contractor: Kevin Kelly
Structural Engineer: The Office of Gordon Polon
Mechanical Engineer: I & N Consulting Engineers

PARAMOUNT LAUNDRY OFFICE BUILDING
7,000 square metres/75,350 square feet
Client: Frederick Norton Smith
Project Team: Eric Owen Moss; Jay Vanos (project associate), Dennis Ige, Scott M. Nakao (project architects)
Main Contractor: Scott Gates Construction Company Inc.
Structural Engineer: Kurily Szymanski Tchirkow
Mechanical Engineer: I & N Consulting Engineers

PITTARD SULLIVAN
15,200 square metres/163,610 square feet
Client: Frederick and Laurie Samitaur Smith
Project Team: Eric Owen Moss, Jay Vanos (project architect), Dennis Ige (job captain)
Main Contractor: Samitaur Constructs
Structural Engineer: Kurily Szymanski Tchirkow
Mechanical Engineer: Fruchtman and Associates

DUTCH DESIGN INSTITUTE, AMSTERDAM
950 square metres/10,230 square feet
Architect: Benthem Crouwel Architekten b.v.
Client: Municipality of Amsterdam
Project Team: Jan Benthem, Mels Crouwel, Ton Liemburg, Heike Löhmann
Main Contractor: Schakel en Schrale
Structural/Mechanical Engineer: GEAM
Quantity Surveyor: GEAM

ERICSSON PALACE CONVERSION, PRAGUE
3,000 square metres/32,290 square feet
Architect/Interior Design: Jestico & Whiles
Client: Perpetum s.a.
Main Contractor: Stamont/Pirea

EUROPEAN HOUSE OF PHOTOGRAPHY, PARIS
3,550 square metres/38,210 square feet
Architect: Yves Lion Architecte
Client: Ville de Paris
Project Team: Yves Lion, Annie Lebot
Collaborating Architects: Alan Levitt

Main Contractor: S.C.G.P.M.
Structural/Mechanical Engineer/Quantity Surveyor: GEC

FLOAT MUSEUM, JOHANA
750 square metres/8,070 square feet
Architect: Benson + Forsyth with Suzuki Architects Office
Client: Fujie-San, Arata Isozaki Architects
Project Team: Gordon Benson, Alan Forsyth, Annabelle Henderson
Collaborating Architect: Tom Heneghan of The Architecture Factory
Main Contractor: Suzuki Architects Office
Consultant: The Urban Factory

GERMAN DESIGN CENTRE, ESSEN
5,000 square metres/53,820 square feet
Architect/Interior Fit Out: Foster and Partners
Client: Bauhutte Zeche Zollverein Schacht XII GmbH
Project Team: Sir Norman Foster, David Nelson, Paul Kalkhoven, Stefan Behling, Reinhard Joecks
Collaborating Architects: Buro Böll und Krabel
Exhibition Design: Design Zentrum Nordrhein Westfalen
Historical Conservation Consultants: German Statutory Historical Bodies
Structural Engineer: Ove Arup and Partners (new construction); Weber, Hamelmann, Surmann (old construction)
Mechanical Engineer: Ingenierburo G. Hoffmann
Quantity Surveyor: Buro Böll und Krabel (cost control)

GRAND CENTRAL TERMINAL DEVELOPMENT, NEW YORK
200,000 square metres/2,152,780 square feet
Master Plan: Beyer Blinder Belle, Architects and Planners
Client: Metropolitan Transportation Authority
Collaborating Architect: Harry Weese & Associates
Consultants: Goldman Copeland Associates (utilities engineers); Jules Fisher & Paul Marantz Inc (lighting); Vignelli Associates (architectural graphics); Shen Milson Wilke (acoustics/PA system); Schirmer Engineering Corp. (code consultants); Frank S. Welsh (historic paint and colour analysis); AMIS Construction (cost estimating)

GRAVES HOUSE, PRINCETON
465 square metres/5,000 square feet
Architect/Interior Design: Michael Graves Architect
Project Team: Michael Graves, Gary Lapera, John Graham, Peter Neilson, Don Menke
Main Contractors: Stoneleigh Corporation (west wing); Nicholas Carnevale (north wing); Duncan Doyle (phase 1)
Structural Engineer: Blackburn Engineering Associates, PA
Mechanical Engineer: John L. Altieri, Consulting Engineers
Landscape Architect: Julie Bargmann

THE HACKESCHE HÖFE, BERLIN
10,000 square metres/107,640 square feet
Architect: Weiss & Faust

Collaborating Architects: Architekturburo von Bohr & Sander; Architekturbüro Leisering
Client: Hackesche Höfe, Berlin GmbH & Co
Developer: Roland Ernst; Rainer Behne
Aedes Gallery: Van Berkel & Bos

HAKODATE BAY REGENERATION, HOKKAIDO
1,705 square metres/18,350 square feet
Architect: Okada & Associates/Architects Engineers Planners
Client: Nippon Yusen Kaisha (NYK)
Project Team: Hokkaido Okada, Shinichi Okada, Shoji Takatsuki
Interior Designer: AXE
Main Contractor: Shimizu Corporation
Historical Conservation Consultant: Shinichi Okada
Structural Engineer: Shimizu Corporation
Mechanical Engineer: Environment Equipment Consultant
Quantity Surveyor: Hokkaido Okada

HOPE CENTER FOR ADVANCED TECHNOLOGIES, DETROIT
67,666 square metres/728,350 square feet
Architect/Interior Design: SHG Incorporated
Client: Focus: HOPE
Project Leader: S. B. Vora
Main Contractor: R. A. DeMattia
Structural/Mechancial Engineers: SHG Incorporated

HOUSE EXTENSION, BUDERIM
120 square metres/1,290 square feet
Architect/Interior Design: Clare Design
Client: Ferre and Mieke Dedeyne
Project Team: Lindsay and Kerry Clare
Main Contractor: Gordon Winch
Structural Engineer: Todd Group

ING AND NNH BANK, BUDAPEST
1st phase: Andrassy Ut
7,830 square metres/84,280 square feet
Architect/Interior Design: EEA Erick van Egeraat Associated Architects b.v.
Client: Nationale Nederlanden Vastgoed
Project Team: Erick van Egeraat, Tibor Gáll, Maartje Lammers, Gabor Kruppa, János Tiba, Astrid Huwald, William Richards
Main Contractor: CFE Hungary Építoipari Kft
Structural Engineer: ABT Adviesbureau voor Bouwtechniek b.v.
Mechanical Engineer: Ketel Raadgevende Ingenieurs bv
Quantity Surveyor: MDA Overseas Ltd.

2nd phase: Paulay Ede Utca
5,000 square metres/53,820 square feet
Architect/Interior Design: EEA Erick van Egeraat Associated Architects b.v.
Client: ING Real Estate International
Project Team: Erick van Egeraat, Attila Komjátih,

Maartje Lammers, Gabor Kruppa, János Tiba,
William Richards, Dianne Anyika
Main Contractor: CFE Hungary Építőipari Kft.
Historical Conservation Architect: Mrs Tahitóth
(monument authorities, Budapest)
Structural Engineer: ABT Adviesbureau voor
Bouwtechniek b.v.
Mechanical Engineer: Ove Arup & Partners International Ltd;
Mérték Építészeti Stúdió
Quantity Surveyor: Munk Dunstone Associates Overseas Ltd

LA LLAUNA SCHOOL, BADALONA
1,800 square metres/19,375 square feet
Architect/Interior Design: Enric Miralles Benedetta Tagliabue
Arquitectes Associats with Carme Pinós
Client: Town Hall of Badalona, Barcelona
Project Team: Enric Miralles, Carme Pinós
Main Contractor: Castells
Historical Conservation Consultants: Office of the
Municipality
Structural Engineer: A. Obiols, R. Brufau

THE LINGOTTO, TURIN
250,000 square metres/2,690,975 square feet
Architect: Renzo Piano Building Workshop
Client: Lingotto s.r.l. .
Project Team: S. Ishida (associate in charge), P. Ackermann,
E. Baglietto, A. Calafati, M. Carroll (test track, landscaping,
south tower, 1994), M. Cattaneo (interiors, 1994), A. Carisetto,
G. Cohen, F. Colle, P. Costa, M. Cucinella (pavilion five, 1987),
S. De Leo, A. De Luca, S. Durr, K. Frasen, A. Giovannoni,
C. Hays, G. Hernandez, C. Herrin, W. Kestel, P. Maggiora,
D. Magnano, M. Mariani, K. A. Naderi, T. O'Sullivan, D. Piano
(completion), M. Rossato Piano, A. Sacchi, S. Scarabicchi
(public floor, hotel, offices 1994), P. Sanso, A. Stadlmayer,
R. V. Truffelli (completion), M. Varratta (fair centre 1992,
concert hall 1994), N. Van Oosten, H. Yamaguchi
Main Contractor: Fiat Engineering, Turin (pavilion five)
Association of Contractors: Recchi, Pizzarotti, Guerrini,
Rosso, Borini & Prono (fair centre)
Consultants: Ove Arup & Partners (concept design);
A. I. Engineering; Fiat Engineering (final design)

LUDWIG FORUM FOR INTERNATIONAL ART,
AACHEN
6,000 square metres/64,580 square feet
Architect/Interior Design: Eller + Eller Architekten
Client: City of Aachen
Project Team: Fritz Eller, Philipp Eller (project partners),
Jürgen Geddert (project architect)
Main Contractor: G. Quadflieg GmbH
Historical Conservation Consultants: Rheinisches Amt für
Denkmalpflege
Structural Engineer: Mathias Kempen
Mechanical Engineer: Huber Ingenieur Technik
Quantity Surveyor: Eller + Eller Architekten

MEDIA CENTRE, HAMBURG
8,410 square metres/90,524 square feet
Architect: me di um Architekten
Client: Procom Investitions und Beteiligungsgesellschaft mbH
Project Team: Jentz, Popp, Störmer, Wiesner, Jentz-Koska,
Lietz, Hulsemann, Wolke, Bracht, Aisslinger, Schuchert, Bilen,
Heinrich, Neubert, Dittmann
Main Contractor: Richard Ditting GmbH & Co. KG.
Collaborating Architect: Dinse, Feest Architekten

MEWS HOUSE, EDINBURGH
80 square metres/860 square feet
Architect/Interior Design: Richard Murphy Architects
Client: Jens and Carol Hogel
Main Contractor: Inscape Joinery
Structural Engineer: David Narro
Quantity Surveyor: Spiero Gumley

MUSEUM OF CONTEMPORARY ART, BERLIN
20,000 square metres/215,280 square feet
Architect/Interior Design: Prof. Josef P. Kleihues, Kleihues +
Kleihues Gesellschaft von Architekten mbH
Client: Senatsverwaltung für Bauen, Wohnen und Verkehr
Project Team: Roger Karbe, Claudia Herscu
Main Contractor: Prof. Josef-Paul Kleihues
Structural Engineer: GSE Ingenieurgesellschaft mbH
Civil Engineer: HI-Technik AG

MUSEUM OF FINE ARTS, LILLE
28,000 square metres/301,390 square feet
Architect/Interior Design: Jean-Marc Ibos and Myrto Vitart
Architectes Urbanistes
Client: Town of Lille
Project Team: Jean-Marc Ibos and Myrto Vitart, Pierre
Cantacuzène (project architect in charge), Sophie N'Guyen
(façades and museography)
Main Contractor: P.M.B. – Eiffel (façades)
Structural Engineer: Khephren Ingéniere; Alto Ingénierie

NATIONAL STUDIO FOR CONTEMPORARY
ARTS, LE FRESNOY
42,000 square metres/452,080 square feet
Architect/Interior Design: Bernard Tschumi Architects
Client: French Ministry of Culture, Region Nord-Pas-de-Calais
Project Team: Bernard Tschumi, Tom Kowalski, Jean-Francois
Erhel, Véronique Descharriéres, François Gillet, Mark Haukos,
Yannis Aesopos, Henning Ehrhart
Main Contractor: SOGEA
Structural Engineer: Tetrserf
Mechanical Engineer: Choulet
Quantity Surveyor: Fouché

NESTLÉ HEADQUARTERS, NOISIEL
63,000 square metres/678,125 square feet
Architects: Reichen & Robert Architectes
Client: Société Immobilière de Noisiel
Project Team: Jacques Lissarrague (project leader);

Florence Robert (landscape architect), Anne Carles-Stefano
(interior designer)
Interior Design Consultant: Bernard Grenot
Main Contractor: Société Bovis s.a.
Historical Conservation Consultant: D. Lefevre
Structural Engineer: Gil
Mechanical Engineer: OTH

OBERBAUM CITY, BERLIN
Client: Sirius Immobilien-und Projektentwicklungs GmbH

Building 1
18,056 square metres/194,350 square feet
Architect: Architekturbüro WEP, Effinger Partner
Main Contractor: Generalbau Englmann & Locker
Mechanical Engineer: Englmann & Locker

Building 2A
25,400 square metres/273,400 square feet
Architects/Interior Design: Architekten Huxoll & Schwab;
Architekten Gotz & Hootz; Architekten Shuh & Hurmer
Structural Engineer: IBF Ingenieurbüro Dr. Falkner GmbH
Mechanical Engineer: Brandi Ingenieure GmbH
Quantity Surveyor: Roland Ernst Städtebau und
Projektentwicklungs gesellschaft mbH

Building 2B
12,900 square metres/138,850 square feet
Architect/Interior Design: Architekt T. v. d. Valentyn
Quantity Surveyor: Hypo-Tecta Immobilienentwicklungs-und
verwaltungs GmbH

Building 3
62,500 square metres/672,740 square feet
Architect: Architekten Schweger & Partner
Main contractor: Arge OBC Building 3/Oevermann/Hochtief
Historical Conservation Consultants: Katharina und
Wieland Geipel
Structural Engineer: Leonardt, Andra & Partner
Mechanical Engineer: Englmann & Locker
Quantity Surveyor: Hypo-Tecta Immobilienentwicklungs-und
verwaltungs GmbH

Building 4
35,000 square metres/376,740 square feet
Architect/Interior Design: Architekten Reichel & Stauth
Main Contractor: Arbeitsgemeinschaft Oberbaum City
Historical Conservation Consultants: Katharina und
Wieland Geipel
Structural Engineer: Leonardt Andra & Partner
Mechanical Engineer: Bohne Ingenieure
Quantity Surveyor: Roland Ernst Städtebau und
Projektentwicklungs gesellschaft mbH

Building 5
17,000 square metres/182,990 square feet
Architect/Interior Design: Architekten Reichel & Stauth

Main Contractor: Tekser Bau GmbH
Historical Conservation Consultants: Katharina und Wieland Geipel
Structural Engineer: Leonardt Andrä & Partner
Mechanical Engineer: Bohne Ingenieure
Quantity Surveyor: Roland Ernst Städtebau und Projektentwicklungs gesellschaft mbH

Building 6
35,800 square metres/385,350 square feet
Architect/Interior Design: Architekten Hilmer, Sattler, Albrecht
Quantity Surveyor: Hypo-Tecta Immobilienentwicklungs-und verwaltungs GmbH

Oxo Tower Wharf, london
61,000 square metres/656,600 square feet
Architect: Lifschutz Davidson Ltd.
Client: Coin Street Community Builders
Main Contractor: Trollope & Colls
Structural Engineers: Buro Happold
Quantity Surveyor: Turner & Townsend

Performance Space, paris
1,000 square metres/10,760 square feet
Architect/Interior Design: Cuno Brullmann s.a. d'architecture
Client: Ville de Paris, Direction de l'Architecture
Project Team: Cuno Brullmann, Arnaud Fougeras Lavergnolle
Collaborating Architect: Daniel Durassier
Main Contractor: Quillery
Historical Conservation Consultants: Architectes des Bâtiments de France
Structural Engineer: Terrell Rooke Associés
Electrical Engineer: Bastin, INEX Ingeniere
Quantity Surveyor: Cabinet Gree le Doit

P.S.1 Institute for Contemporary Art, long island city
12,000 square metres/129,170 square feet
Architect/Interior Design: Frederick Fisher & Partners, Architects
Client: City of New York
Project Team: Frederick Fisher, Joseph Coriaty (managing partner)
Collaborating Architect: David Prendergast & Associates
Main Contractor: Foundation Constructors
Structural Engineer: Silman & Associates
Mechanical Engineer: Mario Molina

Public Library, salamanca
5,254 square metres/56,550 square feet
Architect/Interior Design: Víctor López Cotelo Arquitecto with Carlos Puente Fernández
Client: Ministerio de Cultura
Project Team: Víctor López Cotelo, Carlos Puente Fernández, Javier García Delgado, José Antonio

Valdés, Mark Bulkhalter (interiors)
Main Contractor: Agromán s.a.
Historical Conservation Consultant: J. Alvarez Villar
Structural Engineer: José María Fernández
Mechanical Engineer: Sefri Ingenieros, Crespo & Blasco
Quantity Surveyor: José Antonio Valdés

The Reichstag, berlin
61,166 square metres/658,384 square feet
Architect: Foster and Partners
Client: Bundesrepublik Deutschland
Project Team: Sir Norman Foster, David Nelson, Mark Braun, Stefan Behling
Main Contractors: Rogge GmbH (rendering); Kirchgassener (metalwork); Zublin (shell and core); Waagner-Biró AG (dome construction); Nickel (mechanical works); EAB Wismar (lighting and electrical); Alisch-Therma (kitchen); Dr. W. Studke (certifying engineer)
Historical Conservation Consultants: Acanthus
Structural Engineer: Ove Arup & Partners; Schlaich Bergermann; P. Leonardt Andrä & Partners
Mechanical Engineer: Kaiser Bautechnik; Kuehn Associates; Fischer · Energie + Haustechnik; Amstein + Walthert, Planungsgruppe Karnasch-Hackstein
Quantity Surveyor: Davis Langdon & Everest; Büro Am Lutzowplatz

Retail and Office Development, innsbruck
2,702 square metres/29,084 square feet
Architect/Interior Design: Peter Lorenz
Client: Dr. Hans Rubatscher
Project Team: Peter Lorenz, Hanno Parth, Petra Gritznig, Michael Stoeckl, Manfred Koenig
Main Contractor: Hinteregger KG
Structural Engineer: Wallhofer Mac
Quantity Surveyor: Lochs Wolfram

Tate Gallery of Modern Art, london
34,547 square metres/371,860 square feet
Architect: Herzog & de Meuron Architekten AG
Client: Tate Gallery, London
Project Team: Jacques Herzog, Pierre de Meuron, Harry Gugger, Christine Binswanger (partners in charge)
Collaborating Architects: Shepard Robson
Structural Engineer: Ove Arup & Partners

Temporary Contemporary Museum, los angeles
18,900 square metres/203,437 square feet
Architect: Frank O. Gehry & Associates, Inc.
Client: Museum of Contemporary Art, Los Angeles
Project Team: Frank O. Gehry (design principal), Robert Hale (project principal), C. Gregory Walsh (project designer), Randy Jefferson (project principal, renovation), Edwin Chan (project designer, renovation), Vano Haritunians (project manager, renovation), Chris Mercier (project captain, renovation), David

Kellen, Michael Moran, Tomas Osinski, Sharon Williams
Structural Engineers: Kurily and Szymanski
Mechanical Engineer: Sullivan and Associates
Electrical Engineers: Athans Enterprises

Trust Theatre, amsterdam
2,700 square metres/29,062 square feet
Architect/Interior Design: Mecanoo Architekten
Client: Trusttheater
Project Team: Francine Houben, Chris de Weijer, Michel Tombal, Francesco Veenstra, Ursula Fritz, Gerrit Schilder jr.
Main Contractor: Konst en Van Polen b.v.
Structural Engineer: ABT Adviesbureau voor Bouwtechniek
Mechanical Engineer: Ketel Raadgevende Ingenieurs
Quantity Surveyor: BBN, Houten

BIOGRAPHIES

MARIO BELLINI ASSOCIATI S.R.L.
Piazza Arcole 4, 20143 Milan, Italy
Mario Bellini studied at the Milan Polytechnic. Editor of *Domus* from 1986 to 1991, he has lectured at leading design schools throughout the world and since 1995 has taught at the University of Genoa School of Architecture. Completed projects include the office building of the AEM Thermoelectric Power Plant at Cassano d'Adda; the Milan Trade Fair Extension; the Tokyo Design Centre; the Schmidtbank Headquarters in Germany; the new Arsoa Company Headquarters in Yamanashi-ken; and the Natuzzi Americas Inc. Headquarters in North Carolina. Bellini is also well known for his exhibition design, working on shows such as 'The Treasury of S. Marco in Venice' at the Grand Palais in Paris. He has been involved in product and furniture design since 1963: examples can be seen in design collections including that of the Museum of Modern Art in New York.

BENSON + FORSYTH
37d Mildmay Grove North, London N1 4RH, UK
Professor Gordon Benson and Alan Forsyth both graduated from the Architectural Association in 1968 and have been partners for over 20 years. Notable built schemes include the the Divided House in Oshima, Japan and the Jyohanna Museum also in Japan. They are currently working on the Museum of Scotland and the Wordsworth Trust Library.

BENTHEM CROUWEL ARCHITEKTEN B.V.
Weerdestein 20, 1083 GA Amsterdam, The Netherlands
Benthem Crouwel Architekten was founded in 1979 by Jan Benthem and Mels Crouwel who both studied at the Technical University of Delft. Their practice is involved mainly with public work in the fields of urban design, utility buildings, offices and museums. Notable projects include the AHOY Exhibition Centre; the West Terminal at Amsterdam Schipol Airport; and the Museum Nieuw Land at Lelysted. They are currently working at Schipol Airport on a railway station and World Trade Centre.

BEYER BLINDER BELLE ARCHITECTS & PLANNERS
41 East 11th Street, New York, N.Y. 10003, USA
Beyer Blinder Belle is internationally recognized for their expertise in historic preservation and adaptive reuse and has restored large-scale public buildings including the New York Historical Society and the Enid Haupt Conservatory. They are also involved in retail design and have completed the flagship store for Liz Claiborne on Fifth Avenue. The firm came together over 30 years ago and has since received numerous prizes, including the 1995 Firm Award from the American Institute of Architects.

CUNO BRULLMANN S.A. D'ARCHITECTURE
13 rue Gracieuse, 75005 Paris, France
Cuno Brullmann graduated from the Swiss Federal Institute of Technology in Zurich and worked for Ove Arup Associates and Renzo Piano, and was project architect at Piano and

Rogers for the construction of the Pompidou Centre in Paris from 1974 to its completion. Brullmann's architectural practice was formed in 1983 by Brullmann and Arnaud Fougeras Lavergnolle. Today, the practice works both in the public and private sectors. Schemes include the CANVA system for the city of sciences at La Villette in Paris; the St Louis Polytechnic at Cergy in Pontoise; as well as numerous housing projects and shopping centres.

CLARE DESIGN
P.O. Box 5010 Maroochydore South, Queensland, Australia 4558
Lindsay and Kerry Clare both trained at the Queensland University of Technology and opened their own practice in 1979. Their mix of modernism and traditional Queensland architecture has earned them over 22 state and national awards from the Royal Australian Institute of Architects for housing, public recycling, civic and commercial projects. They are currently working as Design Directors for the NSW Government Architect. Recent projects include the Sydney Cove Waterfront Strategy; the Royal Botanic Gardens Exhibition Centre; the Sydney Olympic Village School; and the Environment Centre for the Riverina Institute of TAFE.

GUILLERMO VÁSQUEZ CONSUEGRA ARQUITECTO
Laraña 6, Seville 41003, Spain
Guillermo Vásquez Consuegra graduated from the School of Architecture in Seville. The majority of his schemes are museums, local government buildings, social housing and institutions. He is currently Professor of Architecture in Navarra and Almeria universities.

VÍCTOR LÓPEZ COTELO ARQUITECTO
Pasaje de Doña Carlota 8, 28002 Madrid, Spain
Víctor López Cotelo worked both in Germany and in Madrid before starting his own practice in 1979. His has received much acclaim for his projects, which include the Institute of Architects in Burgos; the town hall in Valdelaguna; the Palacio de Linares; and the public library in Zaragoza. In 1994 his refurbishment of the Casa de las Conchas received three awards. He is currently professor of the Technical School of Architecture in Munich.

ELLER + ELLER ARCHITEKTEN GmbH
Cecilienallee 40, 40474 Düsseldorf, Germany
Eller & Eller was founded in 1959 and over the next few years won placings in numerous architectural competitions. At this time Eller + Eller were mainly active in the fields of school and university buildings. The company has gone through many changes of leadership and today has offices in Berlin, Leipzig and Moscow as well as sister companies, Diete and Partner (construction/project management) and Eller Maier Walter International (commissions in the Russian Federation). Today the practice undertakes commissions in a variety of areas including administrative and public buildings. Fritz Eller is Professor of Construction Design at Aachen Technical

University. In 1994 he was appointed to the advisory board for the new government buildings in Berlin.

FREDERICK FISHER & PARTNERS, ARCHITECTS
12248 Santa Monica Boulevard, Los Angeles, California 90025–2518, USA
Frederick Fisher studied art and art history at the Oberlin College and architecture at UCLA. He founded Frederick Fisher & Partners in 1980 and is well known for his design, art and cultural spaces as well as his innovative residential schemes. His collaboration with David Ross in 1982 and Joseph Coriaty in 1987 resulted in larger commissions: today they work throughout America, France, Germany, Japan and China. For the past six years he has been the chair of the environmental design department at Otis/Parsons.

FOSTER AND PARTNERS
Riverside Three, 22 Hester Road, London, SW11 4AN, UK
Sir Norman Foster studied at the University of Manchester and at Yale University. He established Team 4 in 1963 – with his late wife Wendy and Su and Richard Rogers – and founded Foster and Associates in 1967. Today, he is internationally known for his high-tech designs, such as the Hongkong and Shanghai Bank (1979–86) and Stansted Airport (1981–89). Notable schemes include the Sackler Galleries in London; the Carré d'Art in Nîmes; the Cambridge Law Faculty; the Commerzbank in Frankfurt; and Chek Lap Kok Airport in Hong Kong which, covering an area of 1,248 hectares is the largest project in the world. Norman Foster received a knighthood in 1991. His work has received over 140 awards and citations.

FRANK O. GEHRY & ASSOCIATES, INC.
1520-B Cloverfield Boulevard, Santa Monica, CA 90404, USA
Frank Gehry studied architecture at the University of Southern California and city planning at Harvard University's Graduate School of Design. He established his own practice in 1962 and has since worked on public and private buildings in America, Japan and most recently in Europe; projects include the Vitra Furniture Manufacturing Facility and Design Museum in Germany; the American Cultural Centre in Paris; and the Guggenheim Museum in Bilbao. He won the Pritzker Architecture Prize in 1989 and has been named a trustee of the American Academy of Rome. A major retrospective exhibition of his designs was organized by the Walker Art Centre in Chicago in 1986, which then travelled within the United States. Recent schemes include a mixed-use building adjacent to the Brandenburg Gate in Berlin; the Samsung Museum of Modern Art in Seoul, the Nationale-Nederlanden Building in Prague, the EMR Communication and Technology Centre in Bad Oeynhausen and the Vitra International Headquarters in Basle.

MARCO GOETZ KATRIN HOOTZ ARCHITEKTEN
Backerstrasse 57, D-81241, Munich, Germany

Marco Goetz and Katrin Hootz went into partnership in 1990. The practice is involved with smaller public buildings and residential schemes. They are currently working on a branch of the Bayerischen Bank, Nurnberg, and a renovation and extension of offices in Munich.

TEODORO GONZÁLEZ DE LEÓN ARQUITECTO
Amsterdam 63, Mexico DF 06100, Mexico

Teodoro González de León trained in Mexico City before being awarded a scholarship by the French Government. From 1947–48 he worked in the studio of Le Corbusier where he was involved in making blueprints for the Unité d'Habitation in Marseilles. On his return to Mexico, he formed his own practice and has worked on both domestic and large-scale public and private commissions. In collaboration with Abraham Zabludovsky he has completed the Site Museum in Chichén-Itzá and the Mexican Embassy in Brazil, with Francisco Serrano. Further schemes with Serrano include the public library in Brazil as well as the Administrative and Financial Centre for the Mexican Embassy in Berlin. He has recently completed the Mexican Gallery at the British Museum in London.

MICHAEL GRAVES ARCHITECT
341 Nassau Street, Princeton, New Jersey 08540, USA

Michael Graves received his architectural training at the University of Cincinnati and Harvard University. Since the formation of his practice in 1964, he has produced designs for over 200 projects. Through his affiliated company, Graves Design, he has worked on an extensive collection of furniture and consumer products, collaborating with manufacturers such as Alessi, Baldinger and Atelier International. Major architectural schemes include the Walt Disney Swan and Dolphin Hotels, Orlando; the Disney Company Headquarters in Burbank, California; the Whitney Museum of American Art in Johnstown; the Denver Public Library; the corporate headquarters of Thomson Consumer Electronics in Indianapolis; and the World Trade Exchange Centre in Metro Manila in the Philippines. He is the Schirmer Professor of Architecture at Princeton University, where he has taught since 1962.

HERZOG & DE MEURON ARCHITEKTEN AG
Rheinschanze 6, 4056 Basle, Switzerland

Jacques Herzog and Pierre de Meuron began their partnership in 1978, and along with Harry Gugger and Christine Binswanger, founded their current practice in 1997. Today they have offices in Basle, London and Munich. Both Herzog and de Meuron are visiting professors in architectural practice at Harvard University and are members of the Association of Swiss Architects and of German Architects. Award-winning schemes include the Signal Box and the Engine Depot in Basle. They are currently working on the Tate Gallery, Bankside in London.

HODGETTS + FUNG DESIGN ASSOCIATES
1750 Berkeley Street, Santa Monica, California 90404, USA

Founded in 1984, Hodgetts + Fung Design Associates comprises Hsin-Ming Fung and Craig Hodgetts. Hodgetts is a professor at UCLA's School of Architecture and Urban Planning. He received his Masters in architecture from Yale after which he worked for Sir James Stirling and Robert Mangurian. Fung is associate professor at the California State Polytechnic University School of Environmental Design. Since working together they have completed many award winning schemes including the Towell Library, UCLA; the California State Archives Museum; and the Craft and Folk Art Museum, Los Angeles. Most recently they have been awarded the 1994 Architecture Award from the American Academy of Arts and Letters and the 1996 Chrysler Award for Innovation in Design.

ARCHITEKTEN HUXOLL & SCHWAB
Hauptstrasse 4, 82008 Unterhaching, Germany

Huxoll & Schwab was founded by Huxoll over 30 years ago. He has recently left the company to act as a freelance consultant. The practice is involved in all aspects of building development.

JEAN-MARC IBOS AND MYRTO VITART ARCHITECTES URBANISTES
8 Impasse Druinot, 75012 Paris, France

Jean Marc Ibos and Myrto Vitart were associate members of Jean Nouvel & Associés. They set up their own practice in 1989, since which time they have received many national prizes including one for the Museum of Fine Arts in Lille. Other notable schemes include the School of Architecture in Tours, the Notre Dame de la Pentecôte church in La Défense and the First-Aid Centre for the Nanterre Fire Department.

JESTICO & WHILES
14 Stephenson Way, London NW1 2HD, UK

Jestico & Whiles was founded in 1977 by Tom Jestico, John Whiles, Robert Collingwood and Tony Ingram and today has offices in London, Glasgow, Prague and Munich. The concept of low-energy work spaces features strongly in their design philosophy: recent work includes embassies and ambassador's residences in Latvia, Bulgaria and Bratislava.

PROF. JOSEF P. KLEIHUES, KLEIHUES + KLEIHUES GESELLSCHAFT VON ARCHITEKTEN MBH
Holsterbrink 12, D-48249, Dülmen-Rorup, Germany

Prof. Josef P. Kleihues founded an office in Berlin in 1962, and in 1973 founded his second office in Dülmen-Rorup. He is currently the Professor for Architecture at the Kunstakademie, Düsseldorf. Recent work includes the Museum of Contemporary Art in Chicago as well as urban developments for the cities of Berlin, Groningen, Pforzheim, Santiago de Compostela and Turin.

LIFSCHUTZ DAVIDSON
Thames Wharf Studios, Rainville Road, London W6 9HA, UK

Lifschutz Davidson was formed in 1986, the partners having

met when they were both employed by Norman Foster's practice to work on the Hongkong and Shanghai bank. They have designed private and community housing, supermarkets, a power station, a railway station for Crossrail, offices, bridges and are at the moment commissioned to carry out a large urban improvement scheme for London's South Bank.

YVES LION ARCHITECTE
29 bis rue Didot, 75014 Paris, France

Yves Lion studied at the École des Beaux-Arts and worked as a photographer for six years. He set up his own studio in 1974, after working for various architectural practices in France. Since 1973 he has worked periodically with Alan Levitt who is now a permanent partner in his firm. They are well known for their renovation schemes, most notaby the conversion of redundant offices into domestic spaces. Yves Lion has been professor at the École d'Architecture Paris-Tolblac from 1987 and is also visiting professor at the University of Quebec in Montreal and at the University of Karlsruhe.

PETER LORENZ
Maria Theresien Strasse 37, Innsbruck, A-6020 Austria

Peter Lorenz was born in Innsbruck in 1950 and received a Masters degree in architecture from the University of Venice. He has had his own practice since 1980 and today has offices in Innsbruck and Vienna. He has completed over 200 projects ranging from housing schemes, retail outlets and offices and has recently undertaken city planning and large urban schemes. He is a lecturer at various universities and frequently holds workshops and study trips worldwide.

MECANOO ARCHITEKTEN B.V.
Oude Delft 203–2611 HD Delft, The Netherlands

Mecanoo was founded in 1982 by a group of young architects who won an architectural competition for the Kruisplein in Rotterdam. Today the practice is involved in a wide range of urban design, including social and commercial housing projects, residential schemes, interior design, restoration and landscape design. Their works include the public library at Almelo; the Isala College, Silvolde; and the Faculty of Economics and Management at Utrecht University.

ENRIC MIRALLES BENEDETTA TAGLIABUE ARQUITECTES ASSOCIATS
Ptge Pau 10 bis Pral., 08002 Barcelona, Spain

Enric Miralles formed his current practice in 1990, along with his partner Benedetta Tagliabue. The firm is involved with architecture, interior design and facility planning and over the last nine years has gained experience in educational, residential and restoration schemes as well as landscape design. Most of their clients are from the public sector. Miralles has received numerous awards including the National Prize of Spanish Architecture in 1995 and the Gold Lion at the Venice Biennale in 1996. Notable schemes include a social centre in Madrid; a pavilion for the Tateyama Museum in Japan; and the park and cemetry in Igualada

Barcelona. Miralles worked with Carme Pinós between 1984 and 1989.

ICHIRO MIZUNO + KANAZAWA PLANNING RESEARCH COMPANY LTD.
6F Spring Point Building, 1-66-1 Nishiizumi, Kanazawa, Ishikawa 921-8043, Japan
Ichiro Mizuno founded Kanazawa Planning Research Company in 1980. He graduated from the department of engineering at the University of Tokyo and the Tokyo University of Fine Arts in 1966. He began teaching at the Kanazawa Institute of Technology in 1977 and is currently chair of the department of architecture. Recent commissions include the Nanao Fisherman's Wharf and the lecture hall at the Kanazawa Institute of Technology.

ERIC OWEN MOSS ARCHITECTS
8557 Higuera Street, Culver City, California, 90232, USA
Eric Owen Moss opened his office in 1973 in Los Angeles. Since then, he has gone on to receive 35 design awards. Current projects include work in Vienna, Spain, France, New York, Los Angeles and Culver City. Forthcoming work includes the high-rise towers in Los Angeles and the Stealth Building in Culver City. Moss's work has been exhibited widely.

RICHARD MURPHY ARCHITECTS
34 Blair Street, Edinburgh, EH1 1QR, UK
Richard Murphy formed his practice in 1991. Murphy's various domestic renovations have received national awards and the Fruitmarket Gallery in Edinburgh gained an EAA Commendation, a RIBA Award and the Civic Trust Commendation. He has written monographs on Carlo Scarpa and Charles Rennie Mackintosh.

OKADA & ASSOCIATES/ARCHITECTS ENGINEERS PLANNERS
2-35-5 Hakusan Bunkyo-ku, Tokyo 112, Japan
Okada & Associates was established in 1969 by Shinichi Okada who graduated from the University of Tokyo. Recently completed schemes include the Okayama Prefectural Museum of Art, the Hakodate History Plaza and the Miyazaki Prefectural Art Museum.

PIETRO CARLO PELLEGRINI ARCHITETTO
Via di Poggio 34, 55100 Lucca, Italy
Pietro Carlo Pellegrini studied at Rome and Pescara universities. He opened his studio in 1985 and has since completed numerous restoration schemes including the Cathedral Museum of Lucca; the Museum of Beata M.D. Brun Barbantini in the historical site of the Suore Oblate Congregation in Lucca; and the bee-keeper's house and laboratory in Ponte a Moriano. He is currently working on 40 apartments in Lucca and the restoration of the west wing of the Ferrero Lamarmora Palace.

RENZO PIANO BUILDING WORKSHOP
via P. P. Rubens 29, 16158 Genoa, Italy

Renzo Piano graduated from the School of Architecture at Milan Polytechnic in 1964. He worked with Louis Kahn in Philadelphia and Z. S. Malowski in London, before collaborating with Richard Rogers, Peter Rice and Richard Fitzgerald. In 1981 he established the Renzo Piano Building Workshop and today has offices in Genoa, Paris and Osaka. Recent projects include Kansai International Airport; the Potsdamer Platz Urban Redevelopment; Cité International in Lyons; the Science and Technology Museum in Amsterdam; and the Mercedes Benz offices in Stuttgart. He was awarded the 1998 Pritzker Architecture Prize.

ARCHITEKTEN REICHEL & STAUTH
Frankfurter Str. 4, 38122 Braunschweig, Germany
The architectural practice Reichel & Stauth is based in Berlin and is active in the fields of office and public buildings, hotels, entertainment centres, accommodation, town planning and restoration of industrial quarters. It is currently working on blocks 4/5 of the Oberbaum City in Berlin.

REICHEN & ROBERT ARCHITECTES
17 rue Brézin, 75014 Paris, France
Reichen & Robert was founded in 1973. The company has developed an international reputation for sensitive renovation projects such as the textile mill refurbishments in northern France and the conversion of la Grande Halle de la Villette and le Pavilion de l'Arsenal in Paris. Its recent rehabilitation of the Menier chocolate factory which now houses the Nestlé headquarters was awarded the MIPIM in 1996. New-build schemes include the American Art Museum in Giverny, the French Embassy in Qatar and the Environmental Technology Centre in the Ruhr.

RICHARD ROGERS PARTNERSHIP
Thames Wharf, Rainville Road, London W6 9HA, UK
Richard Rogers founded his practice with John Young, Marco Goldschmeid and Mike Davies in 1977. Their work has ranged from low-cost industrial units to prestigious headquarters; from technical laboratories to landscape proposals; from cultural centres to office developments and from airport planning to the restoration of historic monuments. Their most notable schemes include the Pompidou Centre in Paris and the Lloyd's building in London. Recent projects number the European Court of Human Rights, Strasbourg and the Headquarters Building for Channel 4 Television. The practice is currently working on the Fifth Terminal at Heathrow and the extension of Terminal One. Richard Rogers received the RIBA Royal Gold Medal for Architecture in 1986, and a knighthood for services to architecture in 1991.

SAMYN AND PARTNERS ARCHITECTS AND ENGINEERS
Chée de/Stwg op Waterloo, 1537, B-1180 Brussels, Belgium
Samyn and Partners was founded in 1980. Such projects as the National Bank of Belgium, the Forestry Centre at Marche en Famenne and numerous town-planning and housing schemes demonstrate Samyn's preoccupation with form and

material. Philippe Samyn studied at the Massachusetts Institute of Technology and at the École de Commerce Solvay and has been Principal Lecturer of Applied Sciences at the Free University of Brussels since 1984.

REGINA SCHUH
Regierungsbaumeister Architektin, Viktoriastrasse 9, 80803 Munich, Germany
Regina Schuh established her practice in 1988. She is now involved with commerical, administrative and residential projects. She is currently working on Block 2 (155 residential units and carparking) at the Oberbaum City in Berlin.

ARCHITEKTEN SCHWEGER & PARTNER
Valerinskamp 30, 20355 Hamburg, Germany
Schweger & Partner was founded in 1964 and became Architekten Schweger & Partner in 1987 when Peter Schweger formed a project team for the purpose of designing the technical college in Hamburg-Bergedorf. Recent schemes include the Parliament Building, Bundesrat in Berlin; the headquarters of the Deutsche Bauindustrie, Berlin; an industrial park development in Potsdam; the Promotion Park in Bremen; and Halle 14 Messe for Hannover Expo 2000.

SHG INCORPORATED
150 West Jefferson Avenue, Suite 100, Detroit, Michigan 48226, USA
SHG is the oldest continuously practising architectural and engineering firm in the USA. It specializes in the design of corporate headquarters, laboratories, manufacturing centres, hospitals and academic buildings. SHG has offices in California, Arizona, Michigan and Washington as well as branches in Malaysia and the Philippines.

SUSSMAN/PREJZA & COMPANY, INC.
8520 Warner Drive, Culver City, CA 90232, USA
Deborah Sussman opened her first architectural practice in 1968 in Santa Monica. In 1980 Sussman/Prejza was incorporated with offices in Culver City. The company is involved with large-scale public schemes, designing retail, sports, convention and performing arts centres throughout America. Clients include Walt Disney World, Euro Disney and the City of Philadelphia. In 1984 it was commissioned to develop the visual appearance of the Summer Olympic Games in Los Angeles. Sussman/Prejza is a women-owned enterprise.

BERNARD TSCHUMI ARCHITECTS
227 West 17th Street, New York, NY 10011, USA
Bernard Tschumi Architects was founded in 1982 with the commission for the Parc de la Villette after a major international design competition. Recent work includes Columbia University's Lerner Student Centre; the Marne La Vallée School of Architecture; and a Concert Hall and Exhibition Complex in Rouen. Bernard Tschumi has been the recipient of numerous awards including the Legion of Honor-Grand Prix National d'Architecture.

THOMAS VAN DEN VALENTYN

Aachener Strasse 23, 50674 Cologne, Germany

Thomas van den Valentyn studied architecture at the
Staatliche Kunstakademie Dusseldorf and in Vienna with
Hans Hollein. He has been in practice since the early 1980s
and has completed numerous public and domestic projects
in Bonn, Cologne, Hamburg and Weimar. Recent schemes
include the Loggia zum Stadthaus, Bonn; the Juridicum
Martin-Luther-Universitat, Halle; and the Godesberger Allee,
Bonn. He has received national recognition in the form of
various domestic prizes and his work has been published
widely within Germany.

EEA ERICK VAN EGERAAT ASSOCIATED ARCHITECTS B.V.

Calandstraat 23, 3016 CA Rotterdam, The Netherlands

Erick van Egeraat co-founded Mecanoo Architects in 1983
and remained there until 1995, when he set up his own
practice. He has received national acclaim for his designs,
and was recommended for a national award in 1995 for the
glass roof of the Andrassy Boardroom in Budapest. Further
notable projects include the Crawford Municipal Art Gallery
in Cork, Ireland; the Dutch Embassy and apartments for the
Dutch Embassy in New Delhi; the Photographers' Gallery in
London; and the Urban masterplan for Grave in The Hague.

WEISS & FAUST

Schonhauser Allee 40, 10435 Berlin, Germany

Weiss & Faust was founded by Stefan Weiss and Matthias
Faust in 1993. They are involved with residential schemes,
administrative and industrial buildings, culture, sport and
leisure centres as well as interior design.

WEP EFFINGER PARTNER ARCHITEKTEN

Denningerstrasse 13, Munich 81679, Germany

Effinger and Partner Architekten was founded in 1992 and
now has branches in Berlin and Dresden. The practice is
involved with administrative and industrial buildings.

PICTURE CREDITS

INDEX OF ARCHITECTS AND SCHEMES

Published 1999 by Laurence King Publishing

an imprint of Calmann & King Ltd

71 Great Russell Street

London WC1B 3BN

A catalogue record for this book is available from the British Library.

ISBN 1 85669 129 2

Design: state (Mark Breslin, Mark Hough, Philip O'Dwyer)

Divider photography: Jo Lacey

256

Printed in Hong Kong

The author is grateful for the encouragement, advice and expert assistance of Laurence King, Jennifer Hudson, Jo Lightfoot and Jane Tobin at Calmann & King and to the many building owners and architectural practices who have kindly provided pictures and drawings for the book. Among many friends who have made suggestions and helped form the text, he is particularly grateful to Thomas Muirhead.